Timely, Low-Cost *E* in the Public Sector

Christopher G. Wye, *Editor*
U.S. Department of Housing and Urban Development

Harry P. Hatry, *Editor*
Urban Institute

NEW DIRECTIONS FOR PROGRAM EVALUATION
A Publication of the American Evaluation Association
A joint organization of the Evaluation Research Society and the Evaluation Network
MARK W. LIPSEY, *Editor-in-Chief*
Claremont Graduate School

Number 38, Summer 1988

Paperback sourcebooks in
The Jossey-Bass Higher Education and
Social and Behavioral Sciences Series

Jossey-Bass Inc., Publishers
San Francisco • London

Christopher G. Wye, Harry P. Hatry (eds.).
Timely, Low-Cost Evaluation in the Public Sector.
New Directions for Program Evaluation, no. 38.
San Francisco: Jossey-Bass, 1988.

New Directions for Program Evaluation Series
A publication of the American Evaluation Association
Mark W. Lipsey, *Editor-in-Chief*

New Directions for Program Evaluation is published quarterly by
Jossey-Bass Inc., Publishers (publication number USPS 449-050),
and is sponsored by the American Evaluation Association.
Second-class postage rates are paid at San Francisco, California,
and at additional mailing offices. POSTMASTER: Send address
changes to Jossey-Bass Inc., Publishers, 350 Sansome Street,
San Francisco, California 94104.

Editorial correspondence should be sent to the Editor-in-Chief,
Mark Lipsey, Psychology Department, Claremont Graduate School,
Claremont, Calif. 91711.

Library of Congress Catalog Card Number LC 85-644749

International Standard Serial Number ISSN 0164-7989

International Standard Book Number ISBN 1-55542-925-4

Cover art by WILLI BAUM

Manufactured in the United States of America. Printed on acid-free paper.

Ordering Information

The paperback sourcebooks listed below are published quarterly and can be ordered either by subscription or single copy.

Subscriptions cost $52.00 per year for institutions, agencies, and libraries. Individuals can subscribe at the special rate of $39.00 per year *if payment is by personal check.* (Note that the full rate of $52.00 applies if payment is by institutional check, even if the subscription is designated for an individual.) Standing orders are accepted.

Single copies are available at $12.95 when payment accompanies order. (California, New Jersey, New York, and Washington, D.C., residents please include appropriate sales tax.) For billed orders, cost per copy is $12.95 plus postage and handling.

Substantial discounts are offered to organizations and individuals wishing to purchase bulk quantities of Jossey-Bass sourcebooks. Please inquire.

Please note that these prices are for the calendar year 1988 and are subject to change without prior notice. Also, some titles may be out of print and therefore not available for sale.

To ensure correct and prompt delivery, all orders must give either the *name of an individual* or an *official purchase order number.* Please submit your order as follows:

Subscriptions: specify series and year subscription is to begin.
Single Copies: specify sourcebook code (such as, PE1) and first two words of title.

Mail orders for United States and Possessions, Latin America, Canada, Japan, Australia, and New Zealand to:
Jossey-Bass Inc., Publishers
350 Sansome Street
San Francisco, California 94104

Mail orders for all other parts of the world to:
Jossey-Bass Limited
28 Banner Street
London EC1Y 8QE

New Directions for Program Evaluation Series
Mark W. Lipsey, *Editor-in-Chief*

Contents

New Directions for Program Evaluation

A Quarterly Publication of the American Evaluation Association
(A Joint Organization of the Evaluation Research Society
and the Evaluation Network)

American Evaluation Association, 9555 Persimmon Tree Road, Potomac, MD 20854

Editors' Notes

In recent years, the usefulness of program evaluation has become a major topic within the program evaluation community. Several volumes of *New Directions for Program Evaluation* have been devoted to this topic (see, for example, Braskamp and Brown, 1980; Saxe and Koretz, 1982; Bryk, 1982), and the theme of the American Evaluation Association's 1987 meeting in Boston was evaluation utilization. This volume is about the use and usefulness of program evaluation done inside government by government staff, rather than by outside contractors or university personnel.

The volume contains articles from evaluation unit personnel representing all three levels of government. The articles have been arranged in an ascending order of complexity, first addressing local, then state, and finally the federal government. In each case, executive branch papers are presented first, and legislative papers second.

Contributing authors were asked to identify how much calendar time and staff were applied for individual studies, indicate the evaluation techniques used, identify a sample of the programs evaluated, provide two or three brief evaluation examples, and indicate how and by whom their study findings have been used.

These particular government units were chosen because they are relatively active in program evaluation activities. Thus, the reader should not assume that the activities described in each case are typical of the program evaluation activities throughout these three levels of government.

This volume also contains two reports from audit offices: those of Malan at the local level and Brown at the state level. Both reports confirm that *performance* auditing closely resembles the evaluation activities of the city of Charlotte and the state of Virginia as described in the chapters by Elliott and Syfert and by Mahone and Corbin-Howerton. (Audit units are generally located in the legislative branch, though some governments also have executive branch audit units. They also do fiscal and compliance auditing, topics outside the scope of program evaluation.)

What follows are some principal points about the evaluation activities of these levels and branches of government. We will also attempt to contrast this type of government work with program evaluations more typically done under contract by university or private evaluation organizations. Readers are encouraged to examine these case studies and determine the information's contrasts and similarities.

Methodology

Generally, executive branch units require fewer methodologically sophisticated techniques than are usually applied in outside evaluations. These government units are less concerned with achieving rigorous evaluation than academics or outside contractors. None of these government units reported using evaluations with random assignments or anything resembling controlled experimental designs. Some of the authors point out that such options are not practical for them. Typically, these government units find their time horizon (their due dates) too short for such techniques. (With advanced planning, however, governments could occasionally use some form of experimental design.)

Legislative units, including the U.S. General Accounting Office (GAO), undertake only after-the-fact evaluations, never experimental designs. (Legislative units could recommend that the legislature require experimental designs at the time a new program is being funded in order to provide more rigorous evaluation.) These legislative organizations accept that after-the-fact evaluations are their mainstay. Brown notes that the evaluation designs used in her office are as "straightforward and inelegant as possible" in order to accommodate relatively short timeframes and make the results easier to explain to legislators.

Government agencies, especially at the local level, employ techniques that differ substantially from those traditionally used in program evaluation—particularly such industrial engineering techniques as time and method studies. The city of Charlotte applied work sampling techniques to assess the efficiency of street maintenance crews and identify the extent of unnecessary, idle time. King County used time studies to audit its jail intake, transfer, and release processes to determine whether the lengthy waiting lines and delays in its booking process could be shortened. These government agency evaluation units are primarily concerned with efficiency, an aspect of performance that is not usually included in what is commonly termed program evaluation.

All these government units require highly objective and sound procedures that will stand up to scrutiny, not merely subjective, unsubstantiated personal observations. In addition to the engineering techniques described above, they utilize such evaluation tools as samplings and statistical procedures. In Washington, for example, the King County parks maintenance auditors developed procedures using a structured visual inspection quality rating scale to examine county parks. It also analyzed citizen complaints to help assess the extent of park maintenance problems. Similarly, the GAO has added meta-evaluations to its tool bag, a phenomenon Chelimsky labels "evaluation synthesis."

All six individual evaluation units were, by and large, allocated three to ten calendar months of time. The authors were unanimous in their belief that this short time period was needed to dovetail with the budget calendar and annual legislative processes. These units are very sensitive to the schedules and deadlines of the executive or legislative leadership. Chelimsky indicates that her program evaluation division at the GAO (potentially the organization most likely to do extended studies) is attempting to speed up the effectiveness of the evaluation process in order to be more responsive and timely in answering legislative questions. She wants to adopt methods that can produce answers within six to nine months, such as synthesizing the evaluations of existing studies, rather than gathering new original data. Of course, this is useful only when there have been past studies similar enough to the subject about which the legislative sponsor needs information.

Subject Matter and Content of Evaluations

These agencies place considerable emphasis on evaluating program *efficiency* as distinct from program *effectiveness*. (The program evaluation profession could probably more accurately be called "program effectiveness evaluation," whereas government evaluation units often focus on "program efficiency evaluation." (For examples of efficiency measurement in other *New Directions for Program Evaluation* volumes, see Silkman, 1986, and Levin, 1987.) Both the local and state papers focus on such efficiency evaluation questions as identifying optimal staffing patterns and using personnel more efficiently. These evaluation unit reports almost always include estimates of program costs, even if efficiency (for example, the relationship between the amount of input and output) is not directly assessed.

In almost all instances, the executive and legislative branch government units provide not only evaluation findings but also suggestions for program improvements. In effect, they combine elements of both summative and formative evaluation, acting both as program evaluation offices and as policy analysis shops. According to Chelimsky, even the GAO has begun to use "evaluation planning reviews," examining existing evaluations relevant to new legislative *proposals*. Brown emphasizes that Illinois legislative evaluation is both summative and formative. Legislators rarely use evaluations to decide whether a program is to be continued. Rather, evaluation-based legislative audit recommendations are aimed at program administrators and suggest improvements to program components. Brown notes that some state legislative evaluation units, such as New York's Legislative Commission on Expenditure Review, have a policy not to make recommendations. (She also notes that there are at least forty-three agencies doing some form of evaluation in state legislatures; eleven of these perform only program evaluations, while the remaining thirty-two do evaluation along with other activities.)

Sometimes executive branch units also analyze different alternatives. Thus, these offices do not only *retrospective* evaluation but also *prospective* analysis.

Frequently, government units address topics that are much more *operational* in character than topics (programs) evaluated by outside evaluation professionals, who typically take an "overall" approach.

Communication and Utilization of Findings

All six government evaluation reports indicate that their findings frequently affect government decisions and actions regarding the programs evaluated. The institutional setting of these government evaluation units gives them direct access to public officials with the authority to implement changes. But, as noted earlier, many government evaluation topics have been more operational, and perhaps of less substantive importance, than evaluations undertaken by outside organizations.

Government executive branch units emphasize the need to interface effectively with the operating agency personnel whose programs they evaluated, both to obtain data and to increase the likelihood of implementation of evaluation report suggestions. Barkdoll uses the term *networking* to describe the process of developing effective working relationships with "parties interested in the evaluation." In fact, the Virginia Office of Program Analysis, as reported by Mahone and Corbin-Howerton, insists on agency participation on study teams. It also provides decision makers with reports of study progress and works closely with budget analysts to ensure that the studies are implemented and used in decision making.

Barkdoll argues persuasively for developing improved communication techniques among the evaluator and all interested parties. He argues that such working relationships will substantially increase the probability of evaluations having impact. He points to such innovative approaches as the U.S. Food and Drug Administration's use of traveling road shows to present analysis findings and provides an example in which this process helped bring about a major new inspections strategy for the agency. He also suggests the use of portable data processing presentation equipment, using interactive and graphic systems to put points across quickly to many different locations, and offering busy evaluation customers a menu of issues from which to choose (rather than trying to give customers complete, lengthy presentations covering elements of minor interest to them).

Some government authors raised the issue that follow-up is needed on decisions influenced by evaluation findings. The Virginia executive branch unit expressed concern that there is inadequate follow-up to ensure that approved recommendations are actually implemented. The state is beginning to consider ways to remedy this, such as providing formal executive policy direction, executive mandates, and formal compliance reviews.

Conclusion

Government evaluation units at all levels, both executive and legislative, serve a major function in providing public officials with valuable information on past program performance. Compared to outside evaluations, they tend to use less rigorous tools, often apply themselves to more operational topics, have faster turnaround times, and focus more on efficiency than effectiveness issues. Their institutional location gives them ready access to officials in the position to act on their findings.

In no way do these units substitute for the need for more rigorous, outside evaluations focused on major public programs. But they do provide public officials with timely, useful information and should therefore be encouraged and nurtured by the program evaluation community.

Christopher G. Wye
Harry P. Hatry
Editors

References

Braskamp, L. A., and Brown, R. D. (eds.). *Utilization of Evaluative Information.* New Directions for Program Evaluation, no. 5. San Francisco: Jossey-Bass, 1980.

Bryk, A. A. (ed.). *Stakeholder-Based Evaluation.* New Directions for Program Evaluation, no. 17. San Francisco: Jossey-Bass, 1983.

Levin, H. M. "Cost-Benefit and Cost-Effectiveness Analyses." In D. S. Cordray, H. S. Bloom, and R. J. Light (eds.), *Evaluation Practice in Review.* New Directions for Program Evaluation, no. 34. San Francisco: Jossey-Bass, 1987.

Saxe, L., and Koretz, D. (eds.). *Making Evaluation Research Useful to Congress.* New Directions for Program Evaluation, no. 14. San Francisco: Jossey-Bass, 1982.

Silkman, R. H. (ed.). *Measuring Efficiency: An Assessment of Data Envelopment Analysis.* New Directions for Program Evaluation, no. 32. San Francisco: Jossey-Bass, 1986.

6

Christopher G. Wye is the director of the Office of Program Analysis and Evaluation in the Office of Community Planning and Development at the U.S. Department of Housing and Urban Development. He holds M.A. and Ph.D. degrees in history and political science from Kent State University and presidential rank in the Senior Executive Service.

Harry P. Hatry is a principal research associate and director of the State and Local Government Research Program at the Urban Institute in Washington, D.C. He is the author of Practical Program Evaluation for State and Local Governments *(1981) and* How Effective Are Your Community Services: Procedures for Monitoring the Effectiveness of Municipal Services *(1977).*

The Budget and Evaluation Department in Charlotte, North Carolina, has provided evaluation efforts since the early 1970s. The techniques and case studies described in this chapter include a management-by-objectives program, contract evaluations, citizen surveys, and performance auditing using formal industrial engineering practices.

Local Government Evaluation in an Executive Environment

Nancy C. Elliott, Pamela A. Syfert

Charlotte, North Carolina, is a city of 375,000 residents in a high-growth area of the Sun Belt. In the last two decades, Charlotte has experienced a 57 percent population increase and a 119 percent expansion of land area as the result of aggressive annexation policies and liberal annexation laws.

In the early 1970s, the federally funded Model Cities Department in Charlotte developed contracts with many outside agencies to conduct social, health, housing, and educational programs in the Model Cities target area. The development of contract objectives, and the subsequent monitoring and evaluation of those objectives, provided a model for a more objective and informed decision-making process.

At the same time that the Model Cities program was developing an evaluation capability, the city's budget officer was establishing a management-by-objectives (MBO) program. One of the initial steps was to contract with the Urban Institute for assistance in establishing performance measures and objectives. These two efforts—contract evaluation and the initiation of an MBO system—led to the creation, in 1972, of the Budget and Evaluation Department, consisting of a director, secretary, and three staff members.

C. G. Wye, H. P. Hatry (eds.). *Timely, Low-Cost Evaluation in the Public Sector.*
New Directions for Program Evaluation, no. 38. San Francisco: Jossey-Bass, Summer 1988.

Since then, Charlotte has experienced rapid growth and faced an increasing volume of complex issues. The demand for objective assessment of the issues, analysis of options, alternatives, and consequences has grown geometrically. Today, the Budget and Evaluation Department's staff of fifteen provides this information.

Techniques of Evaluation

There are four primary techniques used by Charlotte in its evaluation process.

Objectives Program. Each department has a series of objectives that covers all of its major operating areas. These objectives, monitored three times annually, are used to determine such budget factors as staff approval and service expansion.

Contract Evaluation. Begun in the Model Cities program, continued in Community Development, and expanded to include all city contracts with outside social/cultural agencies, objectives with quantifiable achievements are included in the contracts. Detailed evaluation reports are submitted to the City Council prior to any contract renewals.

Citizen Survey. Biennial surveys measure citizen satisfaction with such major city services as parks and recreation, police, sanitation, and capital projects. Timely questions are added concerning tax increases, priority projects for the capital program, and complaints.

Performance Audit. Formal industrial engineering evaluation techniques are used to chart the active time, travel time and idle time of crew members and job classes to determine the appropriateness of crew size, work assignments, and equipment.

Management by Objectives (MBO)

The MBO program determines the overall framework for the evaluation process in Charlotte. More than 500 local objectives cover all the major activities in all departments. Submitted to the Budget and Evaluation Department as part of the budget process, these objectives reflect the endorsed programs and standards of service delivery (response time, work standards, quality, effectiveness) that the City Council has deemed appropriate for Charlotte's government to provide.

In general, objectives written for city departments measure service delivery in one of two ways: effectiveness or efficiency. Effectiveness objectives determine what portion of a specific community need is being met by the resources allocated to a particular service. Efficiency objectives, frequently measured in terms of response time, determine service quality.

In determining which objective type is most appropriate in a given situation, both the amount of a department's control and the availability of alternatives to the city providing the service are considered. Generally, if the city is providing a service that can also be obtained from the private sector in one form or another, then an effectiveness objective is most appropriate. Given its resources, the city must decide what portion of the total community need it can fulfill and then measure its ability to deliver that service. Other measures of effectiveness include visual rating scales and previous years' achievements.

However, if the city is the sole provider of a service, then an efficiency objective is more appropriate. In this case, the city is responsible for providing all of the needed service and must respond to all situations requiring such service. Therefore, response times are frequently measures (especially in emergency situations) of how well services are being provided to the citizens. Other measures, such as productivity standards, cost comparisons, and citizen complaints, can also be used.

Periodically, departments report on the achievement status of objectives. These reports provide a historical record of the service demands placed on a growing city. These demands are then reconciled with service standards to determine work-load levels, which in turn translate into resource requirements.

The most obvious example of this process is the use of response time objectives, which are commonplace among public safety services. The ability of police and fire departments to respond to emergency service calls within certain time frames readily translates into staff needs and station location models.

Response time objectives are also used among the administrative departments. The ability to respond to legal opinion requests in a timely manner impacts the staff needs of the city attorney's office. The ability to process ordinances in five days sets a priority and service standard for the Budget and Evaluation Department, which in turn impacts staff needs.

As part of the budget process, all objectives are reviewed to determine (1) if all department operations are covered by objectives, (2) if all services provided by the department are necessary, (3) if any objectives are not being met due to increased demand, and (4) if alternative service delivery methods could accomplish the same service delivery at less cost.

Three times annually, each department submits a report outlining the achievement status of the objectives to the Budget and Evaluation Department. Periodically, the back-up data are examined by budget analysts for verification, but for the most part, departments are expected to report objectives achievement accurately and honestly, without frequent or detailed auditing.

Table 1 shows two representative samples of objectives and their reported achievement status. Objectives that are not achieved must be identified and additional information provided, explaining why the objective is not being achieved and what department steps will be taken to improve performance.

Table 1. Police Response and Street Maintenance Objectives

Objective: For police patrols to respond in seven minutes or less
to 90 percent of all emergency service calls.

	5 Months	8 Months	12 Months
Number of calls for service	12,664	20,276	30,882
Number answered in seven minutes	11,587	18,248	28,102
Percentage answered in seven minutes	91.5	90	91

Objective: To maintain a street maintenance productivity standard
of 0.30 man-hours per square yard for skin patching and
1.0 man-hours per square yard for pothole repair.

	5 Months	8 Months	12 Months
Square yards of skin patching	47,894	60,293	105,358
Man-hours required	217,700	334,961	526,790
Percentage of man-hours per square yard for skin patching	0.22	0.18	0.20
Square yards of pothole repair	4,164	5,963	12,109
Man-hours required	5,552	6,934	13,454
Percentage of man-hours per square yard for pothole repair	0.75	0.86	0.90

Twice annually, a report summarizing the achievement status of citywide objectives is prepared by the Budget and Evaluation Department. In these reports to the City Council, each department is clearly identified as having achieved x of y objectives for an achievement rate of z percent. The report describes the highlights of achieved objectives and identifies and explains objectives that are viewed as problem areas. Tables 2 and 3 are examples of department summaries from recent status reports.

The MBO program is the backbone of the evaluation process, clearly stating each department's expectation levels for service delivery and providing feedback/assessment of how well each department is meeting its stated goals on a regular basis.

Contract Evaluation

Each year, the city of Charlotte enters into numerous service contracts with outside agencies. Many of these contracts are precipitated by such federal programs as the Job Training Partnership Act and Community Development. However, numerous other contracts are developed

Table 2. Street Cleaning Objectives Evaluation

Street cleaning achieved two of their four objectives
for an achievement rate of fifty percent.

Achievement Highlights
- 83 percent (objective: 80 percent) of all the sample blocks received a rating of 1 or better on a 5-point scale where 0 indicated Very Clean and 4 indicated Very Littered.

Problem Areas
- 82 percent (objective: 100 percent) of the blocks that received ratings of 3 or 4 (Fairly Littered or Very Littered) were raised to 2 (Fairly Clean) within 1 month.

   Reason for Nonachievement: Routine sweeping of the major thorough-fares did not occur regularly during December, January, and February because the city's street cleaning resources were committed to a leaf clean-up program.

Table 3. Financal Objectives Evaluation

The Finance Department achieved thirty-one of its thirty-seven objectives
for an achievement rate of 84 percent.

Achievement Highlights
- The treasury maintained an investment equivalent of 102 percent of its liquid assets (objective: 100 percent).
- The treasury exceeded the annual return of the "Public Investor 10-Bill Index" (6.40 percent) by achieving an annual return of 7.57 percent on the city portfolio.
- The internal audit section exceeded its 3 objectives by performing 31 financial and operational audits (objective: 28).
- The revenue division maintained a collection ratio of 89 percent of the parking and pet violations issued (objective: 88 percent).

Problem Areas
- Water and sewer payments are being applied to customer accounts, on the same day the payments are received, at a rate of 72 percent (objective: 100 percent).

   Reason for Nonachievement: More personnel have been assigned to lobby collections in order to reduce customer waiting time to 5 minutes or less. This has greatly reduced the amount of staff time available for payment processing. The remaining 28 percent of payments are processed the next day.

with such local service agencies as the Convention and Visitor's Bureau, the Arts and Science Council (an umbrella organization for visual and performing arts organizations), and Victims' Assistance. The City Council receives detailed performance assessments before deciding whether to renew these annual contracts for the following year.

Effective contract evaluation requires that the contracts delineate detailed, quantifiable, measurable objectives. In Table 4, the contract provides for after-school tutoring and a summer activities program for kindergarten through sixth grade students. These contract objectives focus on improving grade level reading and mathematics proficiencies as measured by pre- and poststandardized achievement tests. Additional objectives cover the number of children served, teacher-student ratios, drop-out rates, home visits, and parent involvement.

Following City Council approval, the contractor conducts the program or provides a service to meet the contract terms. City staff serve as monitors for contracts originating in the Community Development, Employment, and Training Departments; staff analysts in the Budget and Evaluation Department monitor the other contracts. Although monitoring frequency may vary according to the contractor's needs, monthly contacts are usually made to review program progress and financial status.

Formal progress reports on the achievement status of contract objectives are submitted on a quarterly basis to the contract monitor, who verifies data accuracy and reviews back-up data if validity questions arise. At these reporting points, any problems regarding potential objectives achievement can be identified and steps taken to remedy them.

Near the end of the contract term, which normally corresponds to the city's fiscal year, comprehensive program reviews are conducted. All quarterly status reports and all financial data are compiled, and summaries of objectives achievements are prepared for City Council review. The City Council's need for accurate data to determine contract renewals is considered more important than having the complete year's data.

To facilitate the City Council's reviews, each evaluation begins with a summary page. Table 5 shows the summary page from the tutoring/enrichment program described earlier in this section.

Table 4. School Contract Objectives

- Increase the educational achievement of not less than 80 percent of the enrolled students by raising the average achievement level one-half month for each month of instruction. Achievement shall be measured by comparing pre- and posttest scores of a professionally recognized, national test.

  a) The pretest shall be administered no later than October 12, 1987.

  b) The posttest shall be administered no later than April 9, 1988.

- Enroll no less than 400 low-to-moderate income, kindergarten through sixth grade students from Five Points, Third Ward, West Morehead, West Boulevard, Grier Heights, and any other eligible census tracts designated by the Community Development Department.

- Maintain a program participation rate of not less than 80 percent.

Table 5. Community Development Department
Program Evaluation Report

Name of Program:	*Gethsemane Enrichment Program*
Period Covered:	*July 1, 1984–March 31, 1985*
Date Prepared:	*May 8, 1985*
Contractor:	*Gethsemane Ame Zion Church*

Summary
- The contract was approved by City Council on June 13, 1984, for $313,320, covering a 12-month period (July 1, 1984–June 30, 1985).
- During its first 9 months, the program served 426 youths in the summer program and 492 youths in the after-school program.
- Program costs were $236,773.77 through March 31, 1985.
- The average cost per youth for the summer and after-school programs was $481.25, or $1.15 per youth per hour.

Major Findings
- The program has met or surpassed all of its objectives.
- The program met 123 percent of its client goals.
- The average increases in academic achievement levels were 5 months in reading and 7 months in math.
- The average daily attendance was 396 in the summer program and 371 in the after-school program.
- The dropout rate for the summer program was 0 percent; for the after-school program, 8 percent.
- The program was conducted in 5 locations.
- The program provided in-school tutoring and/or counseling for students when requested by any of the 39 schools where the students were enrolled.
- 562 home visits and 5 parent workshops were reported.

While formal contract evaluations are routinely used on all large dollar volume, Community Development, Employment, and Training contracts, less complex evaluations are used for nondepartmental contracts (usually $50,000 or less). The latter are written with a Scope of Services provided by the agency, rather than the more detailed performance objectives.

Contract reviews provided to the City Council highlight the agency services stipulated by contract, summarize the agency's performance, and report on how much money was spent. While the information provided in these reviews is less detailed than in contract evaluation reports, it allows the City Council to review which specific services are being paid for and to reaffirm that these services are in keeping with the council's policies, goals, and objectives.

Contract evaluations and the contract reviews have evolved into a routine process for both the contractor and the City Council. For the contractors, the process clearly sets out the city's expectations regarding the services and achievements it wishes to "purchase." For the City Council, it ensures that the city's limited resources are being spent on high-priority services that benefit its citizens.

Citizen Survey

A third method of evaluating the effectiveness of city services is through a biennial citizen survey. Conducted since 1976, these surveys measure victimization rates (true crime, rather than reported crime, rates), citizen satisfaction with parks, recreation, garbage collection services, and citizen priorities for capital projects (coliseums, roads, performing arts centers, and low-income housing, for example).

The initial surveys were conducted in person with nearly 2,000 households, but the cost and the time involved proved prohibitive. Fortunately, the Urban Institute of the University of North Carolina at Charlotte now conducts this survey by telephone and makes this tool available to any nonprofit agency that desires to purchase questions on it. Closed-ended questions cost $150, open-ended questions cost $300. The University provides a random selection of people to be interviewed, employs and trains interviewers, assists agencies in developing questions, conducts the survey, and provides all statistical data tabulation. The University also provides a standard set of demographic questions that agencies may use to cross-tabulate responses. A survey of 650 city residents, which allows an error factor of ±4 percent at a 95 percent confidence level, costs the city approximately $5,000.

Exhibit 1 lists some of the questions the city has asked on alternate years.

Upon completion of the survey, the University provides the city with the frequency tabulation and demographic data. Cross-tabulations of the city questions and demographic variables are also provided. The Budget and Evaluation Department then prepares a written report for the City Council outlining the survey's results and comparing the data to previous surveys when applicable.

The usefulness of such evaluation data is best illustrated by a recent example. In November 1986, the frequency of backyard garbage collection was reduced from twice to once a week. After a settling-in period with the new system, a follow-up citizen survey was conducted and compared with data from previous citizen surveys on the subject. The level of citizen dissatisfaction with the new system was so much higher than under the old system that the experiment was discontinued and the old system reinstated.

Performance Audit

The most complex evaluation methods used by the city of Charlotte involve such formal industrial engineering techniques as timed work sampling crew studies. In the following case study, the Street Main-

Exhibit 1. City of Charlotte Questionnaire

1. During the past twelve months, have the sanitation workers ever missed picking up your trash or garbage?
   —If yes, did you contact anyone in the city about this?
   —If yes, were you satisfied with the way your complaint was handled?
2. As a cost-saving measure, would you support reducing backyard garbage collection from twice a week to once a week, allowing those households requesting it to get twice-a-week backyard pickups for an extra charge?
3. How safe do you feel when using parks or recreational facilities?
4. Which of the following statements best describes how well you think city parks are maintained?
   —Very well maintained
   —Very poorly maintained
5. Which of the following statements best describes your feelings about how city recreation programs are meeting the needs of your community?
   —Meet major community needs
   —Do not meet community needs
6. In relation to your own personal financial situation, would you be willing to pay somewhat more in taxes:
   —To build a new coliseum?
   —To build a performing arts center?
   —To expand the Civic Center?
   —To build new roads and improve existing ones?
   —To construct new parks?
7. In the past year, would you say that crime in your neighborhood has increased, decreased, or remained the same?
8. In the past year, has anyone broken into or tried to break into your home, garage, or other building belonging to you?
   —If yes, how many times did this happen?
   —How many incidents were reported to the police?
   —If not all incidents were reported, what was the main reason for not notifying the police?
   —Of those incidents reported to the police, how satisfied were you with the Police Department's handling of the matter?
   —Has anyone taken or tried to take something from you or a member of your household by force or threat of force?
   —Have you or any member of your household been the victim of a beating, knifing, shooting, or other violent attack?

tenance Division of the Operations (Public Works) Department was studied. The emphasis of this performance evaluation was on crew structure, work assignments, equipment utilization, and work methods in each of eleven different types of crews.

The main portion of this audit was conducted in the field with the crews. The data was collected through a work sampling procedure. Work sampling was used to determine the portion of work time that could be classified as "productive" (employees actively engaged in work-related activities) and "nonproductive" (idle time). Work sampling is based on the theory that the greater the number of observations made, the more closely the results will duplicate reality. The number of observations is determined by the degree of accuracy and confidence level desired; for this study, ±5 percent accuracy and a 95 percent confidence level were selected. These accuracy and confidence levels required that approximately 400 observations be made on each of the eleven crews.

Two hour blocks of time were drawn for each crew and matched with a random drawing of days of the week. Two sample periods were drawn, one in the summer and one in the fall, for a total of six observation weeks. Four staff analysts from the Budget and Evaluation Department conducted the observations.

With the help of the street maintenance radio dispatcher, the analysts met the crews at their work site at the appropriate time drawn in the sample. Initial contacts with the crew chief determined who was working with the crew on any particular day, and any deviations from the formal crew assignment (extra staff or too few staff) were noted.

Using the recording sheet shown in Exhibit 2, observers recorded the number of active and idle workers by job classification during two-minute intervals, using a stopwatch for accuracy. If any equipment was active, an appropriate note was made in the equipment active column. The "notes" column was used to explain idle time, note travel time, record when trucks left and returned to the job site, and any other pertinent information.

When the observation periods were completed for all eleven crew types, the data was tabulated. All time was accounted for in one of three categories: active, idle, or travel. Active, idle, and travel time was broken down by each job class, and when possible, the reason for idle time was identified.

Two additional data tabulations were made for most job classes. The first included the number of crew members, by job class, present during each observation period. It was found that the personnel on job sites frequently did not match the formal organizational structure of a particular crew. It was apparent that these variations had to be considered before drawing conclusions based on the crew studies. For example, it was found that crews with high idle time among equipment operators sometimes had an extra equipment operator. When that crew had the correct number of equipment operators, idle time was reduced.

The second data tabulation included the number of observations taken when all the members of a job class on a site were active. These figures had an important bearing on the nature of recommendations. For example, if a crew was found to have 50 percent idle time, it was important to note how the idle time was spread among the observations. If half of the observations showed all of the laborers idle, the probable conclusion would be that the task required all of them, but that the planning and scheduling of jobs, materials, and equipment needed improvement.

Exhibit 2. Crew Study Observation Form

Day: Date: Time: Observer:

Crew Type and Number: Crew Size:

Crew Present:

Notes:

	Active				Idle				Equipment	
#	LAB	EO	MSN	CC	LAB	EO	MSN	CC	Active	Notes
1										
2										
3										
27										
28										
29										
30										

Working Environment and Notes:

But if all of the observations showed half of the laborers active and half idle, then the probable conclusion would be that the crew was overstaffed.

The results of these studies are written and presented to the department. Nearly all of them have resulted in recommendations to reduce crew sizes, improve equipment utilization, and provide the basis for the development of work standards.

Conclusion

Since the inception of the MBO program fifteen years ago, the evaluation of Charlotte's services and programs has been a high priority for city management and policymakers, a commitment that has evolved and strengthened over the years. Evaluations have benefited the city through improved service delivery, increased productivity, and a high level of confidence about the decision-making process.

Although it is difficult to transfer programs from other cities, successful experiences can provide ideas on how to make evaluation useful in other local governments. Charlotte has continuously experimented with various approaches and evaluation techniques to meet the needs of its decision makers. These approaches have included a citizen survey, the MBO program, performance audits, and contract evaluations. In some years, more emphasis was placed on performance audits; in other years, more resources were devoted to contract evaluations. The MBO program has provided the continuity of year-to-year service and program measurement, while other approaches have added depth to the process.

Evaluation information has been presented in as timely a fashion as possible. Charlotte management has learned that it is more important to have *some* information at the time a decision needs to be made than it is to have a comprehensive evaluation report *after* the decision was made. Charlotte made a strong commitment to support and improve the evaluation process, a commitment that continues to be essential to making evaluation routine throughout all levels of city government.

The evaluation staff's high-quality work has helped to establish credibility for the use of evaluation information in decision making. Reports presented to decision makers have been clear, simple to read, and to the point, concentrating on findings and recommendations. The Charlotte experience has demonstrated that long, complex reports are not read and are therefore not as valuable as summary reports.

The evaluation process has consistently focused on questions of resource allocation. How are resources being used? What is being accomplished? Are services being delivered effectively and efficiently? If evaluation can help decision makers with answers to these questions in a timely manner, then the usefulness of the program is self-evident.

As the needs, issues, and priorities in Charlotte change, the continuing success and usefulness of the evaluation process will depend on the city's ability to adapt to those changes.

*Nancy C. Elliott is assistant director of the Budget and
Evaluation Department of Charlotte, North Carolina. She holds
a B.S. in mathematics from Wake Forest University and an
M.S. in family and child development from Kansas State
University.*

*Pamela A. Syfert is assistant city manager and former director
of Charlotte's Budget and Evaluation Department. She has
been responsible for the preparation of the operating, capital,
and objectives budgets, the evaluation of departmental
programs, and special studies for the city manager's office.
She holds a B.A. in history and political science from Cornell
College and an M.A. in political science from Michigan State
University.*

This chapter discusses evaluations conducted in King County, Washington, during the time the author was King County's auditor.

Local Government Evaluation in a Legislative Environment

Roland M. Malan

King County, Washington, is a city of approximately 1,350,000 residents; there are twenty-two incorporated cities within its boundaries. Seattle, home of the county seat, is the largest, with a population of a little over 500,000. The 1987 combined county budget was $545 million. The county employs over 5,000 full-time employees, has sixteen major departments, and provides unincorporated county areas with police service, park and recreation opportunities, and county road construction and maintenance, among other services. Additionally, the county provides court services, maintains a correctional facility, conducts public elections, assesses personal and real estate property values, and prosecutes both civil and criminal cases for its incorporated and unincorporated areas.

The King County auditor, appointed by a nine-member legislative body, is responsible for conducting or instigating financial, compliance, and performance audits on all county operations and any organizations receiving county funds. For the last decade, the auditor's office has had

The author's views and opinions do not necessarily reflect the official policy of the King County auditor's office or the New York State Comptroller's Office.

C. G. Wye, H. P. Hatry (eds.). *Timely, Low-Cost Evaluation in the Public Sector.*
New Directions for Program Evaluation, no. 38. San Francisco: Jossey-Bass, Summer 1988.

an allocation of nine to ten full-time professional positions, which are divided evenly between financial and performance personnel. Six to twelve audits are conducted in any given year, depending upon the work's complexity and the legislative branch's demand for such nonaudit services as analytic support for its annual budget review and policy analysis for county council committees.

Performance Auditing Defined

The King County Auditor's Office regularly conducts evaluations within the context of their audits, a process they call "performance auditing" but which is also known as management or operational auditing. Local government auditors (Malan, Fountain, Arrowsmith, and Lockridge, 1984, p. 9) have defined performance auditing as

> a systematic process of objectively obtaining and evaluating evidence regarding the performance of an organization, program, function, or activity. Evaluation is made in terms of its economy and efficiency of operations, effectiveness in achieving desired results, and compliance with relevant policies, laws, and regulations, for the purpose of ascertaining the degree of correspondence between performance and established criteria and communicating the results to interested users. *The performance audit function provides an independent, third-party review of management's performance and the degree to which the performance of the audited entity meets pre-stated expectations.*

Thus, the auditor uses recognized methods and procedures in an orderly fashion to analyze and make recommendations about events that have already occurred. Most audits are retrospective in nature.

Performance auditing activities fall into two categories: economy/efficiency and program effectiveness. Economy/efficiency refers to the economic, efficient use of resources; program effectiveness refers to how well the entity has achieved its objectives. Therefore, *performance* includes both management's accomplishments and the processes by which they were achieved. It is called *auditing* because it reports on previous events leading to current circumstances, because of its systematic, objective approach, and because it conforms to professional auditing standards.

Professional Auditing Standards

Professional credibility is based on competence and performance. Performance auditing conforms to an established set of explicit professional standards. The American Institute of Certified Public Accountants (AICPA) has developed a comprehensive conduct framework and a standardized process for financial audits, and the U.S. General Accounting

Office (GAO) has extended these rules to performance auditing in its *Standards for Audit of Government Organizations, Programs, Activities, and Functions, Proposed Revisions* (U.S. Comptroller General, 1987). The AICPA's audit standards are included in the GAO's standards and both must be followed when financial audits are performed in conjunction with performance audits.

Independence. Audit organizations are required to be free of any personal, external, or organizational impediments that might interfere with or compromise their work. In cases where an auditor does not meet this standard, it is expected that they will refrain from accepting the audit work. The independence standard also requires that both the auditor and the audit organization be objective in the performance of their professional tasks.

Internal Control Reviews. Internal control evaluations are critical in performance auditing, as weak internal controls are a major source of fraud, theft, and similar illegal acts. It is important to remember that a primary function of auditing is to report to top management regarding how organizational assets are accounted for, the efficiency and effectiveness of their use, and whether they are at risk or have been diminished through illegal means.

Other Relevant Standards. Other generally accepted government standards that apply to performance auditing include the following:

- Auditors assigned to an audit should collectively possess adequate professional skills for the task.
- Due professional care should be taken in conducting the audit and preparing related reports.
- The work should be adequately planned.
- A compliance review should be made of the laws and regulations applicable to the specific audit objectives.
- Sufficient, competent, and relevant evidence should be obtained, providing a reasonable basis for the auditors' judgments and conclusions, and a written record of their work should be retained.
- Auditors should be alert to situations or transactions that could be indicative of fraud, abuse, or other illegal acts, and if such evidence exists, should extend their work to identify the effect of such illegalities on the entity's operations and programs.
- Written reports should be prepared on each government audit.

Failure to conform to these standards results in substandard audits and serious professional consequences.

Value and Practicality of Performance Auditing

Routinely, performance audits call for change, and in most cases, the audits must be publicly released. Audit recommendations can range from minor procedural changes to sweeping organizational ones that might include the replacement of key management personnel. As those recommendations are based upon accurate objective evaluation, performance auditing is often viewed as potentially threatening to key administrative personnel and elected government officials whose reelection campaigns may be adversely affected.

Correctly done, performance auditing conducted in a political environment is not a political activity. To prevent the audit function from becoming a possible political tool for auditors, elected officials, or management, performance auditing should be established either in the entity's charter or through the enactment of a local ordinance that provides it with direction and protection.

Virtually every function, process, segment, activity, or organization in a governmental entity is subject to performance auditing, if performance auditing as defined by the U.S. Comptroller General (1987, pp. 1-5, 1-6) is so broad that it is only limited by the complexity of the jurisdiction within which it resides.

Organizations and Their Responsibilities. Any governmental organization that needs and can afford performance auditing is relatively complex. It will have several departments, each of which contains a series of subunits that may be organized functionally (for example, administration, recreation, maintenance, and capital construction within a park department) or geographically (for example, geographically located health clinics providing services to the community). Each subunit may have further subdivisions. Performance auditing can examine any of the programs, activities, processes, or functions within any department, unit, or subunit. Moreover, it can examine any program, activity, process, or function that cuts across organizational lines (for example, examining capital budgeting process activities, which include requesting capital improvements, the entity's overall administration and its budget organization). In middle- to large-sized municipalities, the potential for performance auditing specific issues is nearly limitless.

Performance Audit Categories. As described earlier, performance auditing falls into two categories: economy/efficiency and program effectiveness. Every program, activity, process, or function managed by the entity can undergo an audit oriented toward one or both of these categories. The work's scope can be broad (examination of the entity's cash management) or narrow (examination of the cash-handling processes of personal property tax receipts).

Components of Performance Audit Categories. Every organizational program, activity, process, and function is subject to management oversight. As managerial practices are integrated into an organizational scheme, they too become auditible. As Malan, Fountain, Arrowsmith, and Lockridge (1984) point out, each economy/efficiency and effectiveness audit can include such entity components as plans and objectives, organizational structure, policies and practices, systems and procedures, controls and control methods, personnel resources and physical environment, staffing practices, and fiscal analysis.

Clearly, the range of performance auditing activities is extensive; specific activities, groups of related activities, individual processes and functions, and management performance all fall within performance auditing's scope. Moreover, the authority to conduct this type of examination lies with the auditor and is not subject to agency management approval.

Audit Issues and Their Selection

A compilation of recent work by local government auditors (see Malan, 1987, pp. 11–24) illustrates the range of performance auditing's possibilities.

- An efficiency audit of a police patrol unit's staff needs examined the allocation and scheduling of officers to their various precincts and geographic districts according to specific days and hours. (Savings—$750,000), King County, Washington
- An efficiency audit examined the rental and disposition of property. (Savings—$250,000), Suffolk County, New York
- An efficiency audit examined whether or not real estate tax abatement properties were being returned to the tax rolls when abatement periods expired. (Savings undetermined, but the entity abated $37 million in 1986, and the internal controls were lax), Philadelphia, Pennsylvania
- An efficiency/effectiveness audit examined a fire prevention inspection program. (Savings undetermined, but substantial problems were found with inspector productivity and inspector management control), Kansas City, Missouri
- An efficiency/effectiveness audit examined a city procurement program. (Savings undetermined, but it was found that blanket purchase orders would reduce costs), Independence, Missouri
- An efficiency/effectiveness audit examined Emergency Medical Services funding allocation and service delivery. (Savings undetermined, but the audit information will be used when the program's next levy support issue is set up), King County, Washington
- An audit examined the policies and procedures that ensure medical care continuity for emergency patients who are subsequently transferred to a mental health facility for psychiatric evaluation. (Savings undetermined), Milwaukee County, Wisconsin

- An effectiveness audit examined the uniformity of residential real estate assessment levels. (Savings undetermined, but the audit determined a lack of uniformity and a regressive tax collection), King County, Washington
- An efficiency/effectiveness audit examined a jail's intake, transfer, and release (booking) processes. (Savings—none, but the audit recommended a cost avoidance of additional corrections officers), King County, Washington
- An effectiveness audit examined the affirmative action program of the New York State Urban Development Corporation. (Savings—none, but the audit indicated major improvements), Office of State Comptroller, New York.

As audits are not normally performed at the request of the audited entity, agencies about to undergo one often wonder why they have been selected. Many factors influence the decision to select one agency, program, activity, process, or function over another.

Relative Risk and Exposure. Normally, there is great potential for identifying improvements in management, organizational structure, and operating procedures to enhance the economy and efficiency/effectiveness of agencies, departments, and programs that spend large sums of money, manage significant amounts of human and material resources, or are exposed to potential litigation.

Recent Audits or Management Studies. Organizations with previously identified problems are candidates for follow-up audits to determine whether those problems have been corrected.

Lack of Program Information. Organizations that provide little program information and have not been audited recently should be considered as audit candidates. Special attention should be paid to experimental or pilot programs.

Adverse Publicity or Complaints. Programs with a history of controversy or complaints concerning their compliance, economy, and efficiency/effectiveness should be audited to provide updated objective information to management.

Legal Requirements. State or local laws may call for performance audits on a specific cyclical basis.

Significant Environmental Changes. Changes in demographic trends that affect specific programs may indicate the usefulness of an audit, particularly if there has been no apparent programmatic response. Large operating budget increases or decreases, shifting client demands, or increasing capital expenditures are also significant indicators.

Management Problems. Performance audits can help clarify and remedy such problems as high turnover rates, low personnel morale, client dissatisfaction, limited accountability data, and inadequate internal control.

Input from Legislative and Administrative Officials. Legislative and administrative leaders usually have a good perspective on their jurisdictions and can provide valuable insights. However, in order to ensure independence and discourage the politicalization of the audit function, candidate selection should ultimately rest with the auditor.

By considering factors such as these, there is a high probability that selected audit activities will prove relevant to their jurisdictions, providing benefits equal to or greater than their cost.

The Audit Process

There are three phases to a performance audit: preliminary survey, fieldwork, and report development. In the preliminary survey, all information relevant to the audit's preliminary scope is gathered and examined to determine the audit's overall and final scope. The fieldwork consists of gathering and analyzing specific information, as well as testing operating systems and procedures. Report development involves converting the analysis results into a written format.

Performance audits require that report findings be supported by sufficient, competent, and relevant evidence. Included in the audit's workpapers, such evidence should lead an impartial outside reader to the same conclusions as those reached by the audit report's author. The findings should consist of five elements.

- *Criteria.* These are the evaluation standards applied during the audit, the premises or assumptions that link the auditor's logic to objective reality.
- *Condition.* This statement demonstrates as neutrally as possible, the relationship between the audited operations and the criteria standards.
- *Effect.* This element describes any observed discrepancies between the evaluation standards and the audited operations.
- *Cause.* This element attempts to identify those factors which, if removed or altered, would affect change in a predictable fashion.
- *Recommendation.* This statement suggests actions that could be expected to have a favorable effect on the problem studied.

Audit Methodology

The two important facets of audit methodology are data gathering and analysis. Each has its own approaches and each is invaluable to the success of a competent audit.

A variety of categories exists relative to *obtaining data,* and within each category, many techniques are available. For example, if data is gathered by interview, structured, open-ended, or informal interview techniques can be applied, depending on the situation. General categories for gathering data include interviewing observation, surveys and questionnaires, and documented data.

Interviewing. An experienced employee's knowledge of his organization is valuable for evaluation purposes. Employees know their organization's actual procedures and functions, and their perceptions, in part, shape activity patterns. Personal interviews with key employees may provide useful performance audit data and eliminate the time required to dig through printed data. Because interviews depend upon personal perceptions, data collected this way require verification.

Observation. Observation as a data-gathering technique is systematic, objective, and when possible, quantifiable. It may be used to determine how long it takes an employee to perform given tasks, what is involved in reacting to an emergency situation, or how allocated staff time is used.

Surveys and Questionnaires. Well-designed surveys and/or questionnaires can provide statistically valid information regarding program effectiveness and possibly regarding program efficiency, but knowledge of statistical sampling techniques is necessary to obtain valid data this way.

Documented Data. Documented information is found in computer files, manually maintained accounting records, or in specific agency-maintained files. Examples of documented information include:

- Inventories (for example, real estate, capital equipment, supplies, and criminal evidence)
- Assessor/treasurer files
- Capital budgeting and monitoring files
- Performance indicators contained in budget documents and actual performance statistics maintained by the budget agency
- Payroll files with items such as position allocations, salaries, salary adjustments, time in position, position vacancies, accrued vacation time, and accrued sick leave
- Personnel management files (for example, position descriptions, classification, and reclassification information)
- Purchasing files (for example, vendor listings, vendor performance, purchase requisitions in process, outstanding purchase orders, accounts payable, purchase discounts, and payment discounts taken)
- Performance in the form of adopted agency standards (for example, work hours required to rebuild an engine, square feet required by task, or employee responsibility).

Once the data have been obtained, it must be *analyzed.* Selection of the proper analytic technique depends upon the audit's objective and the available data. Some of the techniques used regularly by performance auditors include flowcharting, organizational tables, comparative analysis, alternative analysis, work sampling, and mathematical modeling.

Flowcharting. This technique is used for problem identification. It pictorially traces the flow of an activity, process, set of interrelated decisions, information, or a line of communication from beginning to end. It can take the form of a vertical systems flowchart or a horizontal industrial engineering flowchart; it is a useful mechanism for identifying redundant operations or inefficient "bottlenecks."

Organizational Tables. These tables represent organizational structures as they are envisioned by management. They establish the formal interrelationships between groups and the authority/responsibility relationships within an organization's hierarchy. Analysis of such tables leads to questions regarding span of control, staff size, and the functional relations between units and the public.

Comparative Analysis. Information from the audited entity may be compared, with some caution, to preestablished performance standards, other units within the government, or like organizations external to the entity. Such comparisons are entirely dependent upon the comparison's validity. For example, without considering environmental factors, it would be specious to compare New York City's juvenile delinquency recidivism rates with those of Portland, Oregon. However, when specific, identifiable, relevant variables can be isolated, comparison is a valuable technique.

Analysis of Alternatives. As performance auditors are often required to evaluate management decisions, they should be familiar with quantitative decision-making techniques; occasionally, these techniques are also used to develop audit recommendations. Three of the most useful are: present value analysis, which discounts the entity's future cost or revenue streams so that they can be examined against current money values; life cycle cost analysis, which examines the total operating and capital costs, discounted to the present, of capital expenditures; and benefit/cost analysis, which quantifies both benefits and costs, discounted over the life of the program, to determine if the program's benefit is equal to or higher than its cost.

Work Sampling. Barnes (1968) defines this technique as the systematic study of work systems for (1) developing the preferred work system and method, (2) standardizing a system and method, (3) determining the time required by a qualified and properly trained person working at a normal pace, and (4) assisting in training workers in the preferred methods. It is useful for determining operation efficiency (for example, whether the administration of a large county district court system is adequately staffed, overstaffed, or understaffed).

Mathematical Modeling. This technique uses mathematics to predict such things as how many staff members would be required for a particular workload.

For example, given a municipal government with four police patrol precincts, mathematical modeling allocates sufficient police resources to each precinct, based on each precinct's history of service requests. Subsequently, this theory may be used to identify the number of shifts, and number of officers needed for each shift, in order to maximize the use of police officer time.

Performance Auditing in a Political Environment: Does It Work?

Provided professional government auditing standards are respected, performance auditing not only works, it works to the benefit of top management, elected officials, and most important, the public. Professional standards mean that audit work is performed independently and objectively, without interference from its organizational or political environment. When these requirements have been met the performance audit function has flourished. In these cases, management and elected officials recognized that performance auditing consistently develops means to a more efficient and effective use of public resources. Rather than taking a defensive posture, these official used audit outputs to effect change within their organizations and subsequently claimed credit for the resulting public benefits.

When performance audits prove to be only marginally effective or ineffective, impairments have been imposed somewhere in the auditing function's development. Too often, people in high public office fear that the public will interpret a negative audit report as an indictment against them, resulting in the loss of their position or an encumbancy. When concerns about the release of audit reports shortly before an important election or reappointment result in delayed release dates, the audit's function has been encroached upon. If the audit's release date can be controlled, why not also control its scope or use its findings to put pressure upon a political adversary? At this point, the audit function becomes window dressing, legitimizing the existing official structure. Although auditors who exist in this compromised environment can make some noncontroversial improvements in efficiency and effectiveness, the results fall short of their potential and may give the function a bad name.

Local Government Auditing: Park Maintenance

In 1986, the King County Parks and Recreation Division received an appropriation of $10.6 million, $4.1 million of which was allocated for park maintenance. Their 1986 budget requested an increase of about 37,000 maintenance hours over their 1985 budget allotment. The Parks Divison felt that this proposed increase was their best projection of the work hours necessary for a well-maintained park system. The increase would require an additional annual expenditure of $600,000 to pay for twenty additional full-time staff salaries.

Two issues were raised by the Parks Division in relation to their proposed budget increase. First, they indicated there was public pressure to incease the maintenance level of county parks. Allegedly, this pressure arose because the county park system compared unfavorably to city park systems, most notably Seattle's.

Second, they presented a range of options available for addressing park maintenance level concerns. These options included:

- Keeping spending levels relatively constant while using the existing maintenance plan to set maintenance priorities
- Increasing the maintenance budget, using regular county funding as requested in the budget proposal
- Seeking voter approval to establish a system of Park and Recreation Service Areas. These service areas would have taxing authority of up to $.15 per $1,000 of assessed value to provide additional park maintenance.

In response to these issues, a four-part audit was conducted (see Office of the County Auditor, 1986).

Sampling of Park Maintenance. Visual inspections of sample county parks were conducted to determine the quality of their maintenance. Although it is recognized that quality assessment is a subjective matter, it is important to provide county policymakers with an independent evaluation. The sample parks were systematically inspected once each in May and June; each inspection was conducted by a different auditor. On-site inspections of thirty-four parks, representing a cross section of park types throughout the County system, were completed. The sample parks were selected based on maintenance hours expended in 1984, park type (community, regional, or neighborhood), and geographic location. Park components were rated on a scale of one through five, a score of one to two being good, three to four being fair, and four to five being poor. Rated factors included lawn care (mowing, trimming, edging, and leaf removal); plant care (hedge trimming and weeding); garbage (garbage can litter removal and general litter removal); park buildings (floors, walls, stairs, windows, and fixtures); picnic areas (tables, benches, and barbeques); traveled areas (parking lots, sidewalks, stairs, and paths); play and equipment areas; drinking fountains; fences; court areas; ballfields (baseball, softball, and soccer); trees; brush; restrooms (toilet facilities, wash basins, walls, floors, toilet paper, paper towels, and odor).

The inspection reports concluded that park maintenance levels were good. While additional improvements were possible and would add to the county parks' overall appearance, additional maintenance hours were found to be unnecessary and were not recommended.

Review of Citizen Complaints. To determine the extent to which problems in park maintenance existed, citizens' complaints received by the Parks Division were reviewed and observations from the audit staff's parks inspections were collected.

A review of citizen complaints revealed that the majority fell into one of seven categories:

- Barriers or fences being down or park gates being left open after hours
- Need for trash or debris collection
- Trees needing attention
- Grass or brush needing attention
- Vandalism
- Trees hanging over private property
- Transients sleeping in the park.

No problem pattern was discerned from these complaints and no substantial evidence of public concern with maintenance conditions in general was found. The average number of complaints, about one per park, was considered quite small.

Park inspections were more revealing. The average maintenance quality was found to range from 1.30 (good) for ballfield maintenance to 2.20 (fair) for drinking fountains and plant care. The major reason for the low overall rating of drinking fountains was that several were out of order or were not turned on, a problem more appropriately assigned to the parks' Rehabilitation and Repair Program than to its maintenance personnel.

Comparison with Other Jurisdictions. In preparing their budget request for additonal park maintenance resources, the Park Division conducted a comparison between their own county parks and Seattle's city parks, citing that study's results as their justification for additional personnel. The audit found the comparison's results flawed because the following variables had not been considered:

- Physical and structural characteristics of the parks
- Type and level of park use
- Equipment available and organization of maintenance workers
- Quality level desired
- Budgetary constraints and priorities in that year.

Additionally, the comparison did not address the fact that the Seattle and King County park systems are functionally different. Seattle is a major urban center that serves a large, weekday commuter population. Its parks act as a draw to both regional and national tourism, whereas King County parks are primarily used by local residents. It is also relevant that urban park systems help to offset to some extent the relative lack of open spaces and the population congestion of urban settings.

The audit concluded that the Parks Division's comparison should not be used for drawing conclusions about the maintenance conditions or maintenance needs of its county parts.

Options for Increasing Maintenance Hours. In this element, the audit attempted to identify and analyze cost and effectiveness options for increasing maintenance hours. The identified alternatives fell along a cost continuum ranging from most expensive (regular full-time employees) to least expensive (volunteer programs). The audit team also considered the use of contract services and seasonal, part-time employees. Factors included in the evaluation included the standard time required to clean each restroom, the mix of experienced and inexperienced staff members assigned to the task, and the cost of commuting between county parks for county employees and work crews. Contracting for service turned out to be the least-cost alternative. Another prospective alternative to full-time employment involved asking volunteers to maintain the various ballfields. A survey of ballfield users was used to determine the extent to which organized amateur athletic groups would assist the Parks Division in this regard. The survey indicated that 60 percent of the respondents would assist by performing such chores as field preparation, litter pickup, watering, mowing, and hole filling.

Results. A draft of the audit report was forwarded to the County Executive for review and comment. The Executive responded that the Parks Division should look first at lower cost alternatives to new time positions to increase the level of park maintenance. In particular, the Division should consider the establishment of a volunteer maintenance program and should consider when preparing its 1988 budget request, funding for a volunteer coordinator position, transportation, and the materials/equipment necessary to make volunteer labor effective.

The park maintenance audit took about six employee months to complete and was one of three management audits published in calendar year 1986.

Local Government Auditing: Jail Intake, Transfer, and Release

In mid-1986, King County opened a new $60 million jail with accommodations for about 1,200 inmates. By early 1987, the new jail was plagued with long waiting lines in the reception area, telephone waiting times, and delays in the booking (admittance) process of up to sixteen hours. An audit, initiated at the request of the acting director of the Department of Adult Detention and the chairman of the County Council, was completed in early 1988 (Office of the County Auditor, 1987). The audit focused on the intake, transfer, and release (ITR) section which is responsible for booking, transferring, and releasing inmates. Posts staffed by the ITR section include prebooking, booking, release, central control, floor control, floor officer, intake preparation, check-in guard, cashier, and property room. The ITR section was authorized fifty-one full-time Correction Officer positions in the 1987 budget. The department's objective has been a one to two hour booking process, with a maximum delay of four hours. No time-related criteria had been established for releasing inmates.

Prebooking, Booking, and Release. Studies were conducted to determine the average time required to process inmates in prebook, booking, release, and some other ITR section activities. These time studies were conducted by the audit staff over a two month period, seven days per week, twenty-four hours per day. They indicated that an average booking took about sixteen minutes to process, and an average release about six minutes. Data provided by the computer section of jail arrivals by hour and day during February and March 1987 were used to evaluate the prebook and booking functions. Because information showing the arrival of release documents was unavailable, computer data indicating when the releases actually occurred during these months were used to evaluate the release function.

Data from audit time studies were used in conjunction with booking arrival times and release times to evaluate booking and release staff needs. A queuing model was used to determine the number of staff members needed to process bookings and releases with a five-minute waiting time. (Five minutes was selected as a minimum estimate of delay time. Delay time policies are the prerogative of county policymakers.) Subsequently, a linear programming model was used to determine an efficient ITR Section scheduling pattern. The existing ITR staff work schedule was then compared to the linear programming effort's results. It became obvious that the ITR section's staff scheduling could be improved to better match its work load. The evaluation showed that the first and third shifts were understaffed, while the second shift was overstaffed. The audit report recommended that a redeployment of ITR's present staff would reduce delay times during the first and third shifts, and that the hiring of additional staff was unnecessary.

Managerial Laxity. As is often the case, events that occur during audit field work may require extending the scope of the work. During this audit, several team members noticed the potential for increased efficiency based upon observations of managerial behavior and leadership. Assignment of staff and work prioritization is the responsibility of ITR management.

Correction officers assigned to the ITR section are supposed to be cross-trained, thereby allowing maximum staff assignment flexibility on an as-needed basis. During the audit fieldwork, team members observed that correction officers were not being assigned to critical work-load areas on an as-needed basis. For example, if the booking activity is heavy and the release workload is low, release staff could be assigned to help reduce booking delays. This was not done, although it was clearly essential on a number of occasions. Additionally, it was observed that booking officers were used to relieve other posts (such as meal and coffee breaks), regardless of the booking activity level. This was the result of inadequate supervisory attention combined with lax employee cross-training.

Responding to the draft audit report, the county executive stated that his department concurred with the auditor's findings and had already implemented the audit's first three recommendations that had to do with staff allocation, scheduling, and cross-training.

This audit took about six employee months (three calendar months) to complete and was the county's second publicly released management audit report in 1987.

Conclusion

Although performance auditing is contrained by certain conventions and procedures, program evaluations occur as part of the audit process. In local government, these evaluations have the additional requirement of conforming to the professional standards of the government auditing community. The evaluation techniques discussed in this chapter (surveys, questionnaires, interviews, time studies, observations, mathematical modeling, and comparisons) produced effective analyses of the entities being studied and were integral to the auditing procedures used. All government performance audit organizations are involved in evaluation to one extent or another, and the results of this effort save taxpayers countless millions of dollars every year.

References

Barnes, R. M. *Motion and Time Study, Design and Measurement of Work.* (6th ed.) New York: Wiley, 1968.

Malan, R. M. (ed.) "Local Government Auditor's Newsletter." *Audit Abstracts,* Autumn 1987.

Malan, R. M., Fountain, J. R., Jr., Arrowsmith, D. S., and Lockridge, R. L., II. *Performance Auditing in Local Government.* Chicago: Government Finance Officers Association, 1984.

Office of the County Auditor. *Management Audit: Parks Maintenance.* Report No. 86-3. Seattle, Wa.: King County, 1986.

Office of the County Auditor. *Management Audit: Jail Intake, Transfer, and Release.* Report No. 87-2. Seattle, Wa.: King County, 1987.

U.S. Comptroller General. *Standards for Audit of Governmental Organizations, Programs, Activities, and Functions, Proposed Revisions.* Washington, D.C.: U.S. General Accounting Office, 1987.

*Roland M. Malan is the assistant deputy comptroller in the
New York State Comptroller's Office.*

The Virginia Department of Planning and Budget's evaluation
section was created in 1983 to conduct program evaluations
and special studies for the governor, the governor's secretaries,
and the legislature. Consisting of nine evaluation analysts, an
assistant, and a manager, the section functioned on a budget
of approximately $450,000 in fiscal year 1986–87. By the close
of that year, the section had completed more than thirty reports
that influenced major decisions about program funding,
staffing, and policy direction within each of the state
government's functional areas.

State Evaluation in an Executive Environment: Policy Research Meets Political Reality

John A. Mahone, Lin Corbin-Howerton

The Virginia Department of Planning and Budget's evaluation section has not experienced many of the roadblocks and frustrations resulting from decision makers who overlook study results or prefer anecdotal information or opinion to rigorously prepared evaluation studies. Its studies have had a wide audience, and its major recommendations have been implemented. This success is based on several fundamental standards established by the evaluation section's founders.

1. The section does not generate its own studies. Section assignments come directly from such top state decision makers as the governor, the governor's secretaries, the General Assembly, and the budget director.

2. The section conducts one-time, four-to-ten-month special studies that are scheduled to dovetail with the budget calendar and the presession legislative process. The section has no ongoing monitoring responsibilities, thus freeing it for a new agenda of requested studies each year.

C. G. Wye, H. P. Hatry (eds.). *Timely, Low-Cost Evaluation in the Public Sector.*
New Directions for Program Evaluation, no. 38. San Francisco: Jossey-Bass, Summer 1988.

3. Because of this limited time frame, the section employs methods that are as uncomplicated and cost-efficient as possible to achieve valid, reliable results.

4. The section does not, in the name of objectivity, conduct analyses independent of decision makers and the affected agencies; it encourages agency participation on study teams and works diligently to keep decision makers informed of study progress.

5. Taking advantage of its placement in the budget office, the section works closely with budget analysts to ensure that studies are implemented and used in decision making.

Several of these standards contradict common evaluation wisdom and are controversial in other evaluation settings. But with a great deal of care and attention, the components have combined successfully.

The section has never set its own agenda. Often, when decision makers are unable to formulate evaluation research questions, evaluators attempt to do it for them, ultimately designing a study that the evaluator, rather than the decision maker, wants.

Virginia's evaluation section only conducts studies that have been explicitly requested by the top state decision makers previously mentioned; it does not accept requests from individual agency heads. Much of the section's success is a result of the involvement and commitment of these requestors.

The evaluation section often has more study requests than available staff. To resolve this problem, the budget director has established priorities committing the section to only pressing issues with the biggest impact to the Commonwealth. A number of these were accomplished within one year, and their implementation had significant impact on state services and activities.

Dovetailing with the Budget Calendar

The evaluation section was created to provide discrete, long-term analysis of the Planning and Budget Department's programs and activities. *Discrete* is defined as including no formal, ongoing monitoring responsibilities. The section neither conducts compliance audits of studied activities nor receives progress reports from program administrators on a regular basis. *Long-term* is defined as excluding "brush-fire" studies of three weeks' duration. However, the section is committed to the annual budget calendar and cannot conduct studies that require more than ten months to complete.

Uncomplicated Cost-Efficient Methods

While staff members have a broad range of quantitative and qualitative evaluation skills that can be brought to bear on a study, Virginia's evaluation section believes in keeping its methods as uncomplicated and cost efficient as possible. It is tempting to consider designing an issue's ultimate study, employing the rarest and most complex methodologies. However, there are pressing practical considerations.

The section's ten-month time frame strongly influences the choice of methods. And those that are ultimately applied must serve to convince potentially skeptical audiences. While section research methods are fairly sophisticated, it is in the section's self-interest to choose methods that are no more sophisticated than necessary to maintain a balance between time and resource constraints and the need for objective information. This means that the section cannot perform program effectiveness studies involving experimental designs that follow clients over time, unless accurate historical data exist, which is rare. While such approaches are appropriate for certain studies, decision makers generally prefer good answers in one year's time over perfect answers that require five years' work.

Generally, tight time constraints have not required the section to compromise the magnitude of its data collection and analysis. Sampling procedures ensure randomness and generalizability. Commonly used data collection techniques include questionnaires and structured interviews (in person and by telephone); archival data retrieval; standardized test scores, client record reviews, and accounting/budgeting data; structured observation; and fixed interval/random path work sampling. Analytical methods employed on past studies have included pre- and posttest comparisons, multiple regression, factor analysis, and cost benefit analysis. Other studies may require still other methods. For one study, the team developed and validated a client assessment tool by studying mental health hospital services.

Convergence of Politics and Evaluations

Evaluators often strive for autonomy and separateness from the decision makers, concerned that their studies might be compromised. Public sector evaluators recognize that government operations are, by their very nature, political processes; therefore, they are often concerned about the impact of political environments on the integrity of evaluation studies.

Virginia's evaluation section uses an elaborate process to ensure that requestors and other decision makers interested in a study are interviewed extensively during the study's scoping process. Requestors are briefed on how the study will be conducted and given a review of all the possible outcomes, a cautionary note that they may not necessarily be pleased by the study's findings. In addition, interim briefings are scheduled to inform decision makers of the study's progress, potential findings, conclusions, and recommendations. At the same time, however, the section makes all the final decisions regarding methodology, and the results remain independent of political concerns. For example, the section had told governors and legislators committed to holding down growth in state government that significant staffing increases were needed in specific programs, and had these recommendations accepted and implemented.

A significant but less obvious factor in the section's success is the analytical background of several key members of current and past administrations. These men and women were at one time analysts in the executive or legislative branches of Virginia's state government, the organizational path to the governor and key legislative committees through which our studies must pass. Their analytical experience and ties to the General Assembly make them qualified reviewers and powerful patrons of section studies. These include the governor's chief of staff, the budget director, and several of the deputy secretaries. At the same time, the section has tried to establish credibility and good working relationships with legislative staffs. These executive and legislative relationships have been built on mutual interest in the section's study of specific issues.

The collective role of these players in the decision-making process helps to maintain the section's high methodology, analysis, and result presentation standards. They support analysis objectivity and quality and are willing to use their credibility and influence to support study findings, conclusions, and recommendations, all of which makes them important allies. In a number of section studies, the only precondition for having studies accepted and acted upon was that they be objective and defensible. The support of higher-level government officials, however, is often essential to affecting change.

Outside Participants on Study Teams

The addition of temporary personnel can allow methods to be used that would otherwise not be possible within short time frames. Staff-augmented studies are usually conducted by interagency teams of three to sixteen people, led by a senior analyst from the section.

Whenever possible, at least one member of the team is assigned from the program being studied, or from a staff function (such as research or planning) of the agency responsible for the program. Some evaluators consider the use of agency/program staff on study teams as potentially compromising. However, the Virginia evaluation section has found that it adds needed manpower for data collection, provides ongoing program knowledge and specialization to the project leader and other team members, contributes to interagency consensus on recommendations, and often adds credibility.

Depending on the analysis purpose and scope, additional staff from such central agencies as the Department of Personnel and Training may be requested to participate on the team. Finally, teams may also be assisted by temporary employees or local university research groups. These options have been used to accomplish work sampling and extensive telephone surveys.

Importance of Placement Within a Budget Agency

The section's organizational placement has been advantageous to its studies and their implementation. Generally, studies are completed between March and December of each calendar year, with analysis scheduled to accommodate budget process time constraints. Placement within a budget office provides easy access to top decision makers and is helpful in getting agency and program staff cooperation. In addition, the evaluation section's staff members are able to work directly with agency budget analysts. Often, budget analysts are assigned part-time to a study effort and so have firsthand knowledge of the study's findings and recommendations. The budget staff's involvement provides an ongoing opportunity for study result implementation through subsequent budgets and day-to-day discussions with the line agency. Budget analysts are eager to have reliable program data and analysis to apply to their resource decisions.

Budget analyst involvement in study implementation ranges from detailed discussions to brief, informal hallway conversations. Like the support of top decision makers, it is an important process based on mutual cooperation. Too many stories abound about organizational infighting between evaluation and budget staffs in other federal, state, and local settings for an evaluation section not to realize the importance of these informal relationships with their peers.

The section's studies have been used principally for program improvement and as an aid to resource allocation decisions. Since program improvements are often tied to resource allocations, applied study recommendations on program content, delivery, and management can be used to determine how resources (both dollars and positions) are doled out over two-year periods. This interaction between the section studies and the budget office has been a significant factor in study implementation, particularly since the section does not routinely maintain any continued involvement in the implementation phase.

Section Studies

During its brief history, the section has completed thirty studies. As with most government evaluations, section studies usually incorporate both a retrospective and a prospective component. Their inclusion is due to the decision maker's need for both an assessment of past practices and results and recommendations for future program improvements. Virginia evaluation section projects have included:

- An assessment of current probation services and the feasibility of increasing probation use in Virginia
- A review of the state police's mission and its staff needs
- An assessment of the Virginia Department of Corrections' security function and manpower needs
- A review of currently contracted services and their feasibility in Virginia's Department of Mental Health and Mental Retardation
- An assessment of the commonwealth's use of bonded debt, and potential management improvements
- The organization and staffing of juvenile learning centers in the Virginia Department of Corrections
- The effectiveness of the commonwealth's accounts receivable collection
- A program review of the commonwealth's industrial training program
- The effectiveness of the commonwealth's court fines and fees collection
- A review of the function, staffing, and management of human resources licensing programs.

The section's efforts are best exemplified by their study of the staffing and treatment in Virginia's mental health hospitals and their evaluation of the tax-exempt status of Blue Cross/Blue Shield's Open Enrollment Health Insurance program.

Treatment and Staffing in Adult Geriatric and Psychiatric Facilities. Inpatient psychiatric services are staff intensive and therefore costly. Because of continuing concerns about resource requirements and the level of care being provided in all Department of Mental Health and Mental Retardation (DMHMR) facilities, the 1986 Virginia legislative session requested a study of specific service issues, including staff needs and treatment.

The state's eight psychiatric and geriatric facilities include four comprehensive hospitals, two smaller mental health institutes, and two freestanding geriatric facilities. The study assessed the staff members providing "hands-on" treatment to patients from approximately twenty occupational groups. Registered and practical nurses, psychiatric aides, and mental health workers comprise more than 80 percent of these positions. The remaining positions include physicians, psychologists, social workers, and occupational/activities personnel.

The nine-month study was conducted by five senior and two junior analysts. They were assisted during data collection by four temporary personnel and seven staff members from the DMHMR, and consultants were used intermittently. Administrative support and management input were provided by other sections of the budget office; data entry services were contracted with another state agency. The study's total cost exceeded $200,000, a financial commitment necessary to meet the legislative request for a 1987 General Assembly report, while permitting the use of the major study methods described below.

1. The team surveyed fifty-nine key participants for "best practices" nominations in adult psychiatric and geriatric inpatient treatment programs. Using questionnaires and telephone interviews, the survey identified those programs where a consensus of respondents believed active treatment was being provided in a manner consistent with patient needs.

2. To validate these nominations, clinical consultants with mental health expertise were contracted to review practices and treatment levels and to identify any potential improvements.

3. Intensive work sampling was conducted in thirty-nine wards of seven hospitals to determine and compare the work activities of nurses and aides and to develop staffing allowances for nurse activities. Wards were selected to ensure a proportional sampling of nominated wards and other wards across all programs. This resulted in approximately 50,000 structured observations, resulting in a system-level sampling error of less than 0.5 percent, with a confidence level of 95 percent.

4. A time-log instrument was developed and completed by clinical treatment personnel for ten consecutive working days. The time-log survey was conducted to determine the activities of psychologists, physicians, social workers, and occupational/physical therapists. A total of 3,357 completed time logs were submitted, for a return rate of 89 percent.

5. A survey was administered to elicit information about the individual needs of each patient. This was done to develop physical care and psychological treatment allowances based on individual care levels and to discover opportunities for inpatient census reduction. Clinical treatment staff assessed each patient using a level of functioning scale. The survey generated 2,557 profiles, providing a one-day "snapshot" of the entire inpatient population.

6. In order to understand nursing staff needs, the "relief" component was updated with a random survey of annual, sick, and other leaves used during fiscal year 1986.

7. Finally, eighty-seven structured interviews were conducted with facility and program directors, clinical department heads, and program managers, to systematically gather their observations concerning treatment programs, patients, and staff issues.

The study recommended systemwide staff increases, the delivery improvement of active treatment, and the enhancement of facility management and operations. The major recommendations covered such areas as:

- How to identify, at the ward and program level, the numbers and types of staff needed to implement the best practices and most cost-effective staff configuration for the delivery of treatment services

- How to improve client services through operational improvements and the elimination of operational inefficiencies
- How to make more appropriate use of existing inpatient resources
- How to improve the central oversight of the facility services system, including services staffing and provisions.

The study results were presented to the governor, the secretary of human resources, the DMHMR's commissioner and the General Assembly prior to consideration of the budget bill. Besides providing seventy-five additional positions in one mental health hospital, the General Assembly allocated approximately $1.3 million systemwide for the improvement of active treatment levels through an upgraded mix of nurses to aides.

The DMHMR is currently developing an implementation plan for many of the report's management recommendations and is using the report's staffing recommendations both as the basis for its upcoming biennial budget requests and for the staffing of a new facility. It is interesting to note that past DMHMR studies of similar scope, using considerable in-house resources and consultants, were never used to the extent this one has been.

The Taxation of Insurance Companies. The Virginia legislature requested a study of possible inequities in the tax treatment of insurance companies. Prior to this study, Blue Cross/Blue Shield plans were exempt from the gross premium tax imposed on other commercial insurance plans because they offer a unique "open enrollment" program. This program provides health insurance coverage to citizens regardless of health history, employment status, occupation, or geographical location. Once enrolled, these subscribers cannot lose their coverage due to high utilization of medical services. The company claimed that without a full tax exemption, it could not afford to offer this high-risk coverage.

The study's purpose was to document the number and characteristics of high risk or uninsurable individuals whose health insurance might be jeopardized if Blue Cross/Blue Shield's prepaid health care plans were taxed, to identify the legal and regulatory requirements needed to protect subscribers and policyholders should tax law changes be recommended, and to propose specific tax structure revisions aimed at rectifying inequities in the current tax treatment of insurance companies.

One full-time and two part-time analysts were assigned to the study. In addition, the team contracted with a local university for telephone surveys and computer data analysis. Analysts in two other state agencies provided intermittent support on an as-needed basis. The total cost of the ten-month study was approximately $50,000. The survey's major methods included:

- Random sample telephone surveys of Blue Cross/Blue Shield open enrollment subscribers to determine their medical characteristics, and document any past or present difficulties obtaining insurance from other carriers
- Survey questionnaires of 160 life insurance companies marketing accident and sickness insurance in Virginia, to identify the application approval practices used for individual and small group health insurance and the medical characteristics of persons denied coverage
- Analysis of health insurance claims submitted to Blue Cross/Blue Shield and five other major commercial insurers, to determine whether Blue Cross/Blue Shield did, in fact, insure a higher risk population than other insurers
- Structured interviews with representatives of Blue Cross/Blue Shield and commercial insurance companies.

The study found that while open enrollment comprises a small portion of Blue Cross/Blue Shield's total business, all of their premiums, not just those attributable to open enrollment, were exempt from the premium tax. The study concluded that open enrollment for individuals and small groups, and the related benefits cited by Blue Cross/Blue Shield, did not adequately justify a tax exemption totaling $33 million in 1985 alone.

Still, the team concluded that some preferential tax treatment was justified, and recommended a partial exemption as an incentive for the company to continue its open enrollment program. Draft legislation was developed to expand certain safeguards for continuing and promoting open enrollment, and a tax rate of 0.75 percent was approved by the General Assembly on Blue Cross/Blue Shield's future premium income. It is estimated that $5.4 million will be collected from this tax during fiscal year 1987–88. Other study benefits include:

- A clearer legal definition of "open enrollment" that will allow the state to know what policy type is being subsidized by the reduced tax
- A requirement that Blue Cross/Blue Shield advertise open enrollment twelve times annually
- A requirement that Blue Cross/Blue Shield give the state two years' notice of any intent to eliminate open enrollment, to allow the state time to implement other means of providing this coverage
- A requirement that Blue Cross/Blue Shield report annually to the State Corporation Commission the number of open enrollment subscribers it covers, including income and benefit payments.

46

Utility of Section Studies

While the section likes to feel that its products are useful to state decision makers, the search continues for ways to increase job performance and the probability of study implementation. One way to get the job done more quickly is to write shorter reports; this has been a section goal for the last two years. Decision makers want objective, reliable, accurate information about the issue at hand. If they can be assured through other means—brief presentations or "second opinions" from other staff, for example—that sufficient methodological and analytical rigor has been employed, a lot of comprehensive report documentation can be reduced and the report can concentrate on the major findings, conclusions, and recommendations that matter.

This should not suggest compromises in analysis or necessary documentation. However, decision makers will rarely read a 300-page report; the goal is to prepare reports that will be read and understood by those who will ultimately spearhead their implementation. To this end, section reports try to provide clear analysis and documentation that answers questions with methodological rigor and reliability in less than seventy-five pages. A decision to produce shorter reports can allow more time for data collection and analysis.

Increasing study utility involves both the informal relationships the section has come to rely on for getting study recommendations accepted and new processes by which the section can "institutionalize" recommendations. Sometimes, when major recommendations are mandated for implementation, there is little formal follow-up to ensure implementation impact beyond the first year following a study's release.

Good working relationships between the section and the budget department are weakened by inevitable shifts and turnovers in personnel, as well as by changing priorities and time demands. For this reason, the section is considering the possibility of institutionalized priority recommendations. This could be accomplished by incorporating study recommendations as policy direction within the executive budget guidelines to individual agencies; including them within the Budget Bill follow-up and having agencies with reviewed programs report on implementation, and developing draft legislation, when practical.

Another way to increase study use is to carve out a limited role in the implementation phase. Assistance in drafting and analyzing the legislative consequences of the Blue Cross/Blue Shield study was essential to its being translated into legislative action. Limited implementation assistance is also underway on the mental health treatment/staffing study; one of the core team's principal analysts spends approximately two hours per week helping to establish the study's implementation plan. It is hoped that this kind of limited, continued involvement will not only assist in the implementation of major recommendations, but also enhance the implementation chances of other recommendations that are often overlooked.

A final method of ensuring implementation is a *compliance review*. One was recently conducted by the Public Safety budget section as a follow-up to a study of security and staffing in adult correctional facilities. Selected members of the original team conducted postaudits two years after the original study to assess the extent to which recommended staffing and management improvements had been implemented by the Department of Corrections. The results will be reported to the secretary and legislative budget staff in preparation for upcoming 1988-90 budget decisions.

Conclusion

The evaluation section continues to seek a market studies "niche" that would provide top decision makers with objective, accurate, reliable information on state agency programs, services, and policies. Decision makers need, and have a right to expect, timely information that responds to reasonably defined questions that mesh with budget development and implementation. Not only does this interaction between the section studies and the budget process assist decision makers, it increases the probability of recommendations being considered and decreases the possibility of good studies being overlooked.

In addition to its organizational placement within the state budget office, the section has benefited from good "design" and an effective network of informal relationships. Its design features include a selection process that allows the budget director to help prioritize study requests and a process for conducting studies that involves both top decision makers and agency/program staff members. This process was designed to achieve the fullest possible participation and sponsorship in both the legislative and executive branches of Virginia's state government. Finally, informal relationships—up, down, and sideways—are crucial to both the implementation of study recommendations and to the creation of future studies.

*John A. Mahone is manager of the Virginia Department
of Planning and Budget's evaluation section. He has been
responsible for managing the analysts who lead interagency
project teams for the governor, the governor's secretaries,
and the General Assembly since 1985. His previous positions
with the Commonwealth have included legislative assistant,
budget analyst, policy analyst, and evaluation analyst. He holds
B.A. and M.A. degrees from the University of Virginia.*

*Lin Corbin-Howerton, a senior evaluation analyst in the
Virginia Department of Planning and Budget, is responsible
for policy analysis, program evaluation, and special studies
for the governor, the governor's secretaries, and the legislature.
Previously, she was a planner and program development
specialist with the Virginia Department of Corrections.
She holds a B.A. and M.S. in sociology from Virginia
Commonwealth University, where she also served as adjunct
faculty instructor in the Department of Sociology and
Anthropology.*

State legislatures began recognizing evaluation as an important aspect of their oversight responsibilities in the late sixties. Since that time, evaluation has become an integral part of the legislative process. This chapter delineates such key issues as how the Illinois Office of the Auditor General has addressed legislative evaluation and the challenges and dilemmas evaluators must address to enhance their future effectiveness.

State Evaluation in a Legislative Environment: Adapting Evaluation to Legislative Needs

Judith R. Brown

The development of legislative evaluation corresponded to the proliferation of social programs in the 1970s. It was often used to gauge the effectiveness of new social initiatives with an eye toward enhancing or expanding them. In the 1980s, however, evaluation's focus shifted from measuring the effectiveness of social programs to identifying ways to eliminate or reduce services and to operate government more efficiently.

In 1969 there were three state agencies engaged in legislative evaluation; today, there are at least forty-three. Eleven state legislatures have created separate units that perform only program evaluations, and sixteen have assigned program evaluation responsibilities to other legislative agencies, usually fiscal units. Staff members in these settings are usually called evaluators. Sixteen other states, including Illinois, have established evaluation units within existing audit agencies whose staff members are frequently known as performance auditors (Jones, 1987; Knighton, 1967).

Each of these evaluators has adapted evaluation research methods to fit their perspective legislative purposes and roles. As economic and

C. G. Wye, H. P. Hatry (eds.). *Timely, Low-Cost Evaluation in the Public Sector.*
New Directions for Program Evaluation, no. 38. San Francisco: Jossey-Bass, Summer 1988.

political environments have changed, legislative evaluators have adjusted their approaches, techniques, and scheduling. This chapter discusses some of the issues and circumstances peculiar to legislative evaluation and some of the techniques and approaches used to address them.

Context of Legislative Evaluation

Traditional evaluation consists of two primary types: formative and summative. Formative evaluation produces information that is fed back to improve a program during its development. Often, the program's components are measured to identify overall improvement methods. Summative evaluation is a retrospective review of the entire program's effectiveness. Summative evaluation results are directed toward the decision makers responsible for the program's survival, rather than toward program staff members (Weiss, 1972).

Formative evaluation's goal is improvement, while summative evaluation strives for disclosure. In this sense, the primary purpose of legislative evaluation is summative, despite the fact that its ultimate goal is government improvement. It provides useful, relevant, accurate, objective, and supportable information (that is, disclosures) for legislative decision making.

However, legislative evaluation is also formative. Legislators seldom use evaluation results to decide whether a program is to be discontinued. Indeed, most recommendations are directed to program administrators and suggest program component improvements.

Initially, legislators directed evaluation units to assess governmental program effectiveness. For example, concerned about the effectiveness and efficiency of the state's public assistance programs, Illinois legislators directed a management study of public aid caseworkers. As part of that study, evaluators compared two intake processes to determine whether a newly implemented assembly-line approach was more effective than the former client-based process (it was not). While costs were a consideration, the evaluation's primary purpose was to improve services by streamlining the intake system. Other studies assessed program impact, helping policymakers decide how to allocate resources and whether the programs should be modified, expanded, or curtailed.

As both federal and state tax revenues stabilized and, in real terms, declined, the focus of formative studies shifted from improving services to decreasing them. Evaluators began to examine the effectiveness of financial management rather than of social service programs. Recommendations to program administrators addressed strategies for reducing service costs or for increasing state revenues through better financial management.

Most issues in legislative evaluations are administrative and, thus, require agency action. However, issues that concern broader public policy and statutory matters necessitate legislative attention. In Illinois, about 30 percent of reported issues result in "matters for consideration by the General Assembly." These matters for consideration take two forms. The first suggests technical or substantive changes to laws. The second raises policy issues and, sometimes, suggests alternatives for addressing them.

Legislative evaluators are cautious about their role in defining public policy. Most evaluation units seek to limit their involvement to providing objective, accurate information and are careful not to infringe on the policy-making role of elected officials. Most avoid even the appearance of trying to promote specific policies. Some, such as New York's Legislative Commission on Expenditure Review, make no recommendations. They present the facts and their conclusions but defer to elected officials for solutions. Evaluators in other states, such as Illinois, present policy issues with alternatives for action but do not endorse specific alternatives.

There is, of course, an implicit assumption that both recommendations to agency officials and issues for legislative consideration will elicit some type of response. Legislative evaluation units must strive to achieve a proper relationship between political relevance and professional empiricism through their organization's structure, procedures, methods, and research techniques.

The remainder of this chapter provides, first, an overview of the way this relationship and role is maintained in Illinois and, second, some of the challenges and dilemmas evaluation units face in enhancing their effectiveness.

Illinois Legislative Evaluation Effort

The Auditor General's Office was patterned after the federal legislation that created the U.S. General Accounting Office. The auditor general is appointed to a ten-year term by a three-fifths constitutional majority of the General Assembly. Although the auditor general deals closely with many legislative commissions and committees (particularly appropriation committees), his primary audience is the Legislative Audit Commission.

The Legislative Audit Commission is a bipartisan committee of legislators from both of the General Assembly's houses. It initiates most legislative evaluations and hears all evaluation results. Both the houses and the appropriation staffs can also require evaluations.

Although the auditor general has the statutory authority to initiate evaluations, he has not exercised this option. Instead, he brings significant findings to the attention of the commission so it can enact evaluation directives. This approach helps ensure legislative interest in evaluation topics, thus encouraging the use of evaluation results.

The auditor general's statutory authority is clear in its intent to isolate him or her from partisan influence. Because of Illinois' highly partisan environment, and to avoid the appearance of political influence, contact with legislative and staff members is limited once an evaluation has been authorized.

When a study is completed, the auditor general distributes its evaluation results to the leadership of both houses, members of the Legislative Audit Commission, and the evaluated agencies' officials. Other interested parties, such as media members or special interest groups, may also request all or some reports or report digests. While media members routinely receive report digests and often obtain supplemental information, the auditor general further avoids the appearance of politicizing by declining to issue press releases. Thus, there is a statutory segregation of duties: legislators direct and publicly review evaluations, but the auditor general conducts them independently and releases their results.

Process. Typically, evaluation staff members have backgrounds in public and business administration, computer science, quantitative methods, accounting, finance, communications, and the social sciences. The goal is to staff each evaluation study with an interdisciplinary team whose skills and perspectives best suit the study. Practical concerns, such as staff availability, are equally important in determining assignments.

Staff assignments are based on technical skills and availability rather than on knowledge of a substantive area. Therefore, the first step in any evaluation is to research the evaluation topic and the agency's background. Generally, legislative evaluators conduct background research before contacting evaluatees; thus, most background information is collected from public records (such as the Illinois Revised Statutes), annual reports, published studies, journal articles, books, and other publications.

Once team members have an understanding of the topic at hand, they prepare a survey plan, a systematic strategy for identifying relevant issues and approaches to addressing them. Often as much as 40 percent of the total work effort is spent on the background research and survey phases.

The end product of this effort is an audit program. This includes the research design, which specifies research hypotheses and methods for testing them. It also includes such administrative controls as project tasks, task assignments, time schedules, and budgeted hours. The audit program is the evaluation's blueprint and its primary time and cost-control mechanism. After the audit is completed, it is reviewed and critiqued by a group of evaluators and specialists not assigned to the study. The team uses suggestions from this review to modify the program.

During the evaluation, each team member's work is reviewed and critiqued by an experienced supervisor. Team members with expertise in specific areas (for example, computer or quantitative experts) must explain their work so that a supervisor with less technical expertise can understand it. Although supervisors must have skills broad enough to understand many highly technical concept applications, they also have access to methodological specialists who can assist them.

Senior staff members spend most of their time designing research strategies and drafting evaluation results; staff evaluators participate more in the fieldwork phase, completing each step in the research design and carefully recording their findings.

Generally accepted government auditing standards must be adhered to; all tests and conclusions must be fully and clearly documented. As a result, evaluation papers include not only interview notes, file search notations, and similar information, but also explanations of why tests were (or were not) conducted, discussions of research technique discussions, and notes on each conclusion's probable reliability. Although confidential during the evaluation, all such papers (unless statutorially confidential) are public property after the reports are released.

The initial report draft is examined by a second independent review team to ensure that appropriate techniques were used and defensible conclusions reached. They review it for logic, clarity, organization, and presentation. After making any necessary revisions, the evaluators index each report statement, and an independent referencer verifies that each fact and conclusion is supported by indexed source documents.

At this point, the evaluators and the evaluatee meet for an "exit conference." Evaluators consult with key program staff members throughout the study, and before the final report is released, evaluatee officials review it, discuss its findings with the evaluators, and provide written responses to those findings. Although these responses may address perceived flaws in research design, methodology, or data interpretation, they seldom do. Generally, the evaluation team is able to justify its methods. Most often, the evaluatees respond by providing supplemental information on why problems developed and how they plan to rectify them.

The final document includes an executive digest of the key evaluation findings, the evaluators' recommendations, and the evaluatees' responses; a detailed report, including background information, findings, recommendations, and responses; and appendixes that include the evaluation directive, the complete text of the evaluatees' responses, methodological explanations, and other supplemental information.

This document represents a considerable challenge in effective communications and, ultimately, in evaluation utilization. Most other evaluations are conducted for program administrators or policymakers who are familiar with the evaluated topic. Legislators, however, deal with a multiplicity of issues, and are rarely familiar with the specifics of any one specific area. Thus, legislative evaluators must not only learn the technical aspects and jargon of each evaluation topic but also be able to translate study results into concise, easily understood, nontechnical language. This is one of the most time-consuming aspects of the process.

Last year, the auditor general adopted the U.S. General Accounting Office's POWER approach to report drafting, which differs significantly from the writing typically used by financial auditors and academicians. Virtually all stilted terminology (such as "It is the opinion of the auditors") is replaced by more direct, simplified language (such as "We think"). More important, while audit conclusions are typically reached deductively, the POWER approach presents them inductively, the conclusion preceding its supporting information.

The POWER approach has five primary advantages. First, its format requires that evaluators understand the exact nature and implications of their findings before they write. Thus, fuzzy thinking can no longer be hidden by verbiage in the hope that readers will somehow reach their own conclusions. Second, conclusions must be stated clearly and precisely. Innuendos and veiled implications are unacceptable. Third, easily identified conclusions allow review teams and referencers to verify their support and defensibility. Fourth, since only clarification and support for conclusions appear, unnecessary narratives are omitted. Finally, these factors result in concise, easily read reports that are more likely to be read and implemented than less concise, more complicated ones.

Approaches and Techniques. Audit directives list the general concerns and specific issues, or determinations, to be addressed. The evaluators' first task is to discover the directive's primary concern and then to examine each determination in light of it.

Evaluation approaches and techniques can be divided into two main categories: standard approaches and individualized research designs. Standard approaches are those procedures used in almost every evaluation. For example, staff members always conduct literature and statutory reviews to identify issues, evaluation criteria, other similar studies, legal requirements, and other programmatic parameters. These approaches also examine the program's evaluation efforts and review existing goals, objectives, and appropriateness measurements. Individualized research designs, however, are more specialized and depend upon specific study objectives.

Research Designs. The basic evaluation approach compares what is against what should be. Some of the should-be criteria are fairly specific. Others, such as some statutory goals—public welfare, for example—need to be operationalized. Research designs are structured around hypothesis testing; contrary to traditional practice, however, the hypothesis may be stated as a question. This reinforces the requirement that each "question" be answered directly and specifically.

Research designs are as straightforward as possible, even if inelegant. There are several reasons for this. First, the results are often more powerful than they would be otherwise. Second, the support for the results is easier to explain to legislators. Third, short evaluation time frames often require the simplest strategies possible.

Most designs incorporate several independent tests and measures with the same hypothesis. Often, quantitative techniques (such as regression and discriminate analysis) are used as indicators rather than definitive explanations. A relationship between two variables is seldom the basis for a conclusion. Rather, it is an indicator that more independent testing and analysis should be conducted.

Legislative evaluators can seldom use experimental designs. Contracting time frames have made quasi-experimental designs rare. As a result, causality is often difficult to determine. Cause is usually ascertained by examining the same issue from multiple perspectives; if several imperfect measures indicate the same conclusion, that conclusion is generally considered to be adequately supported.

Data Collection and Analysis. Most data are collected through routine methods: file searches, questionnaires, interviews, and observations. They are then classified into one of three types of evidence: testimonial, documentary, or analytical. Each has a different reliance level.

Often, program staff interviews provide the first data source. Although this testimonial evidence alone is seldom adequate support for findings, it provides leads and corroborating support for other sources.

Documentary evidence—that is, data found in written documents—is considered the most convincing. Thus, most data are obtained through file searches, existing reports, and records. While the use of extant data conserves time and resources, such information (especially data from computerized information systems) must be verified for accuracy and reliability. Sometimes evaluators spend more time verifying existing data than collecting new data.

Otherwise unobtainable information can be elicited through mail, face to face, and telephone questionnaires. Both factual and perceptual data are gathered. Evaluators try to ensure the accuracy of factual information by carefully constructing instruments and by verifying responses whenever possible. Perceptual data are analyzed more gingerly. Only recently have legislative evaluators recognized the value of perceptual information in diagnosing program weaknesses and in gauging a program's impact, use, and public acceptance. This information (as well as other testimonial and documentary evidence) can be manipulated and analyzed to create analytical evidence.

Often, various test results are combined to test a hypothesis. For example, to test how effectively job discrimination charges were processed and resolved, case records (which specified case characteristics, processing time and events, and final case dispositions) were compared against questionnaires sent to statistically valid samples of complainants and respondents.

This information was then compared to the factual information in the case files. The respondents and complainants had agreed to settlements in almost all the cases; agency officials maintained that this proved that both groups were satisfied with the ultimate dispositions of their cases. But in fact, the complainants were rarely satisfied.

Then, the relationships between evidence supporting complaints, case characteristics (for example, race, sex, size of the employers' work force), and case dispositions were analyzed. No relationship between a complaint's support and its disposition was found. There was, however, a significant relationship between case characteristics and their dispositions. It was possible to predict a case's resolution based upon the complaint (sex, race, or handicap) and the size of the respondent's work force.

This analysis used testimonial, documentary, and analytical evidence. Typically, statistically valid random samples of clients and client records were selected. In this instance, the samples were stratified and weighted. Usually, however, simple or systematic random samples are selected. If possible, samples with 95 percent confidence levels and 5 percent confidence intervals are used, although sometimes tolerance levels are increased to 90 percent confidence levels and 10 percent confidence intervals. Increasing tolerance levels reduces the time and resource requirements but it can result in less powerful conclusions. Sampling decisions are examined to ensure that confidence levels are commensurate with the importance of the test results.

While the evaluator's traditional role has been to examine past or existing conditions, increasingly, he or she is expected to determine the potential effects and future impacts of various deficiencies, strategies, programs, and policies. This movement into what was once the domain of economic forecasters and policy analysts has had a significant impact on evaluation methodology. Most techniques has been limited to random sampling, tests of significance, and various regression analyses. Now evaluators employ those basic methodologies along with more sophisticated modeling techniques.

NIU Engineering Program Study

This case study shows how several research strategies and techniques were used to respond to a legislative directive. In January 1985, the Illinois Board of Higher Education approved a new engineering program at Northern Illinois University (NIU). Need and cost concerns led legislators to request a study of the proposed program. Their directive to the auditor general specified several objectives. Among other things, they wanted to determine whether qualified students were being denied entry into existing state engineering programs because Illinois' universities lacked the capacity to accommodate them, and whether graduating engineers were likely to find employment in Illinois.

To address these issues, the evaluators consulted with fifteen public and private Illinois universities. They also consulted with Illinois businesses to assess the current and projected demand for engineering graduates. Using demographic and statistical data on graduate engineers, team members identified trends since 1950 concerning engineer demand, placement, and industry needs.

To estimate the future supply and demand for engineers in Illinois, an economic model was developed and various sensitivity analyses were conducted. The model's supply variables were determined by projecting live birthrates and (using a cohort survival technique) high school graduate numbers. This candidate pool was narrowed by determining the percentage meeting requirements for engineering programs (the primary measure was ACT scores) and the historical percentage of qualified graduates choosing such programs. Ultimately, the number of Illinois' engineering program graduates was estimated. Demand variables were estimated by examining engineering opportunity trends and adjusting them for replacement, economic growth, and new technology.

Four basic scenarios were projected:

1. A base model, which did not include NIU's engineering school and assumed no change in the state's admission policies due to declining enrollments

2. A scenario, which assumed that NIU would not stimulate state businesses to add engineering positions (additional graduates would have to find work outside Illinois) and that NIU enrollment would have no impact on other schools' enrollments

3. A scenario, which assumed that NIU's program would stimulate a growth rate of 0.5 percent and have no effect on other schools' enrollments

4. A scenario, which assumed that students' ACT scores and engineering school applications would increase.

Each scenario was then adjusted for various other economic and demographic factors, and the results analyzed and compared with demographic and testimonial data.

The evaluation's overall conclusion was that NIU's engineering program was unjustified. Even under the most favorable economic and demographic assumptions, NIU's program would add surplus engineers to the Illinois market. It was also found that public and private state universities had room for additional qualified students and that, even without NIU's program, a substantial percentage of Illinois' graduates would have to seek out-of-state employment.

Evaluators traditionally measure their effectiveness by the degree to which their findings are utilized. Using this criterion, the NIU study was not a resounding success. Since the program had received legislative funding before the study began, the evaluation results had little immediate impact.

But using broader criteria, it was very successful. A second, perhaps more important, usefulness measure is the degree to which evaluations effectively raise and clarify issues, thus providing accurate, objective information for legislative decision-making. Legislators serving on appropriation committees are now more aware of how data can be manipulated to support predetermined objectives. Several have requested more independent reviews of agency justifications for new and expanded programs and have instructed their staff members to monitor NIU's program more carefully, in order to ensure its cost-effectiveness.

The way the General Assembly used the results of this study is indicative of utilization trends throughout state legislatures. Although evaluators may gain more immediate satisfaction from promptly implemented recommendations, sometimes it is more useful to define and clarify policy issues than to correct less significant deficiencies.

More complex evaluation issues require either a combination of short- and long-term administrative remedies or legislative consideration. When long-term strategies are necessary to correct deficiencies, both the strategies and program conditions often change during implementation. As a result, it is difficult to accurately assess the degree to which recommendations have been implemented.

Matters requiring legislative consideration seldom delineate specific action. Most such evaluations inform legislators of the problems and suggest possible solutions. When evaluators do recommend specific legislation, it can be hard to directly link the evaluation results to any subsequent legislation. Laws are seldom enacted quickly, so long periods may elapse between the time recommendations are made and their implementation. Thus, legislation may be attributed not only to the evaluation but also to ensuing political, environmental, and administrative factors.

Still, evaluation results must be considered and used. While legislators appreciate information reports, an evaluation unit whose recommendations are not implemented will eventually be considered superfluous and ultimately be abolished.

Utilization should thus be viewed from two perspectives: agency action and legislative information. This view addresses the need for program administrators to use evaluation results in making concrete improvements while acknowledging legislators' constitutional prerogatives in setting public policy.

Implications for Evaluators

The ways in which decision makers use legislative evaluations and the context in which they are used have important implications for how evaluations are planned, conducted, and presented. First, legislative evaluators must view individual programs in the context of state government. Second, if evaluation results are to be used for legislative decision making, they must be presented to coincide with legislative sessions and budget cycles. Third, legislators must have faith in the credibility of evaluation results and in the organization producing them.

Government Perspective. It is possible for a program to be both efficient and effective on its own but to be neither when viewed in a broader governmental context. Almost every research design includes tasks to compare the evaluated agency's programs to similar activities in other agencies. These examinations identify duplication and gaps in services, review the adequacy of programmatic coordination, and assess a program's impact on its clients and on governmental efficiency and effectiveness.

Legislative Cycle. An evaluation's planning and conduct is affected not only by technical and resource considerations but also by external, sometimes antithetical, time schedules. Legislative evaluators must respond to legislative directives. Typically, these directives specify which agencies will be evaluated and the studies' scopes and objectives. Increasingly, they include a reporting date. Even when directives do not specify dates, report distributions must be coordinated with legislative cycles if they are to be used in legislative decision making.

Credibility. Evaluators tend to equate credibility with methodological rigor and expertise. Legislators are seldom so technically inclined. They tend to take these factors for granted until the first time the legislative evaluator releases a "bad" report, that is, a report which is successfully disputed. A legislative evaluation unit may survive one substandard report but will probably not survive two. Thus, although accuracy, reliability, and validity of findings are often unspoken criteria, they remain necessary (if not sufficient) conditions.

Since legislative evaluations often take place in the midst of controversy, evaluators must provide convincing proof for every conclusion. Suppositions, professional judgment, and testimonial evidence are rarely permissible. Thus, evaluators must document not only facts and findings but also the logic and methods which lead to them. The resulting conclusions may be more narrowly drawn than is customary.

Since the way a question is asked can influence its answer, evaluation units have specific policies and procedures to ensure objectivity and to prevent research from being biased by staff members' values or preconceived ideas.

Most legislative evaluation units comply with generally accepted government auditing standards (see Comptroller General of the United States, 1981). These standards provide general objectivity guidelines. Evaluation units supplement these standards with internal controls. In Illinois, independent evaluation teams and technical specialists review each evaluation's scope, approach, research design, and work program. These elements must respond to the evaluation's directive with methodological appropriateness and rigor. It is also common for the evaluated agency to confirm its agreement with the research design's technical validity. To avoid the possibility or even the appearance of political influence, evaluators have minimal legislative contact during the actual study, restricting such collaboration to preevaluation scoping and postevaluation result presentation.

For most decision makers, credibility is closely related to usefulness. While legislative evaluations must be objective and value neutral, their results must be presented for use in a subjective, value-driven political environment. This usually means that complex, interrelated issues must be presented in clearly defined modules. Generally, legislators disdain traditional discussions of how conclusions were derived and the limitations of the analyses. They prefer a direct, action-oriented approach that states the problem, identifies the cause, outlines potential effects, and makes specific recommendations.

Thus, the context, environment, and uses of legislative evaluations raise important issues. Evaluators are confronted with challenges which, while fascinating in the abstract, are frustrating in practice. They must be politically aware yet professionally independent and objective. While staff members must be well grounded in scientific research techniques, they must also be willing and able to adapt those laboratory techniques to less scientific but equally defensible methodologies. Finally, evaluators must produce objective, valid, reliable, and documented results within the constraints necessary for cost-effective, timely results.

Conclusion

Ten years ago, few legislators questioned evaluation costs. Many said that these studies provided them with necessary information for their oversight responsibilities, therefore, the benefits always outweighed the costs. In today's cost-conscious environment, such beliefs are being reexamined. Increasingly, legislative evaluators are being pressured to do more with fewer resources.

Since legislative evaluations are initiated externally, evaluators must allocate whatever time and resources are necessary to address legislatively determined objectives. However, as evaluation units and legislators continue to work together, the evaluation process becomes more and more focused and cost-effective.

Evaluation results are being used more widely than ever before. Legislative evaluations are providing recommendations not only to improve agency management and effectiveness but also to enhance public policy. Perhaps the greatest challenge legislative evaluators face is preserving their unique role in a profession whose traditional approaches and techniques are being reevaluated to accommodate the demands of a changing world.

References

Comptroller General of the United States. *Standards for Audit of Governmental Organizations, Programs, Activities, and Functions.* Washington, D.C.: U.S. Government Printing Office, 1981.
Jones, R. "Keeping an Eye on State Agencies." *State Legislatures,* July 1987, pp. 20–23.
Knighton, L. M. *The Performance of Post Audit in State Government.* East Lansing: Michigan State University, 1967.
Weiss, C. H. *Evaluation Research.* Englewood Cliffs, N.J.: Prentice-Hall, 1972.

Judith R. Brown is assistant auditor general for program quality in the Illinois Office of the Auditor General. She holds a B.A. in political studies and an M.A. in public administration. She is a member of the Public Productivity Review*'s editorial board, president elect of ASPA's Section on Management Science and Policy Analysis, past chairperson of the National Conference of State Legislature's Legislative Program Evaluation Section (LPES), past editor of LPES* Reports, *founder and editorial board member of* The State Evaluation Network Newsletters, *and co-convenor of the Annual Conference of Evaluation and Accountability.*

The impact, speed, and cost-effectiveness of an evaluation can be increased by building a network of working relationships and by selecting the best method of communicating evaluation results.

Federal Evaluation in an Executive Environment: Two Programmatic Principles

Gerald L. Barkdoll, Douglas L. Sporn

"We do work that is quick, of high quality, and inexpensive" was one consulting firm's advertising motto. However, the fine print at the bottom of the page stated that "clients may select any two of the three." This chapter will not start with a promise that requires small print disclaimers. It will simply describe two principles that evaluators at the U.S. Food and Drug Administration (FDA) have developed through years of experience; these have proven effective in increasing the ultimate impact, timeliness, and use of low-cost, short-term evaluations both from the clients' and the evaluators' perspectives.

These principles state that (1) selecting the right form of communicating evaluation results may mean the difference between a successful and an unsuccessful evaluation, and (2) building a network of working relationships with all of the parties affected by the evaluation is an investment that may pay substantial dividends.

The organization within which these principles were developed, FDA, is a scientific, regulatory agency responsible for carrying out diverse national public health functions. These include the premarket review of all prescription drugs and many medical devices; the inspection of firms

C. G. Wye, H. P. Hatry (eds.). *Timely, Low-Cost Evaluation in the Public Sector.*
New Directions for Program Evaluation, no. 38. San Francisco: Jossey-Bass, Summer 1988.

engaged in the production of foods, drugs, and other consumer products; and research to help identify and quantify any risks associated with the actual or potential use of various consumer and medical products.

The agency's evaluation function is carried out by a small staff in the commissioner's office. At any one time, between six and nine analysts can be found assessing the FDA's domestic food inspection program or developing improved indicators to help forecast changes in the agency's new drug review process, among other studies.

FDA evaluators are interested in finding ways to conduct successful, short-term evaluations, though they are not unique in this regard. Increasing the probability of success will appeal to any evaluator or analyst who has experienced the frustration of completing a first-class piece of work that goes unused and unappreciated. Of course, no amount of "networking" and "fancy communicating" will turn a shoddy piece of analytical work into an evaluation with impact. The two principles described below presume that the analyst has high-quality evaluation skills, a dedication to assisting program managers improve their programs' effectiveness, and adequate knowledge of the programs being evaluated.

Communication: Selecting the Right Form

Successful evaluators must deal with two important evaluation dimensions. First, they must deal with the task being done. The *task dimension* includes the analytical, methodological, substantive aspects of a study. Second, they must deal with the *process dimension*. This includes the nature, timing, and sequence of evaluation activities. The process dimension is usually complex, often difficult to accurately monitor, and frequently complicated by role conflicts and preexisting relationships. Although evaluators may not be in control of all of the factors that determine the process dimension, they do have a great deal of control over communication. They must not only complete the analytical job at hand but also select the most effective way to communicate with clients and stakeholders throughout the evaluation's term.

Communicating evaluation results has gone through three rather well-defined phases at FDA, and each new phase was accompanied by a great deal of discussion and debate. In retrospect, however, it is obvious that the phases were simply evolutionary points on a continuum.

Formal Documentation and Presentation. The formal documentation and presentation phase was a kind of "one-two punch" developed in response to several environmental and historical factors. For example, agency evaluators were intent on establishing a reputation for technical competence and professionalism and proving that they were no longer functioning as investigators or critical auditors. This evolution, and the reasons for it, are described elsewhere (Barkdoll, 1980) and will not be repeated here. A professionally written report (complete with intra-staff peer review) was required as proof of technical competence.

This kind of formal documentation was almost always preceded by an evaluation finding's presentation consisting of conclusions and recommendations to the agency head (who had commissioned the evaluation), the bureau director, and the program manager. A single, formal presentation using large charts was the agency head's preferred style. The three-month time frame imposed on evaluation teams was simply too short to accommodate the formal writing of a report prior to the chart presentation, although it was expected that each evaluation would eventually be "documented."

This "one-two punch" approach to communicating results proved too inflexible to survive the changes in agency leadership and the increasing demands for more useful evaluations.

Optional Presentation. The next phase involved the increased use of presentations, with less emphasis on formal documentation. The increase was needed to deal with such changing factors as:

1. The increased scope, complexity, and duration of the evaluations. This factor necessitated that stakeholders be kept informed about evaluations over much longer periods of time.

2. Multiple clients (rather than only the agency head) commissioning evaluations and research studies. These clients often shared their program responsibility with other powerful managers who needed to be engaged in the evaluation. Frequently, it was ineffective to conduct single, large audience presentations involving all the stakeholders.

3. A decision by the evaluation staff to increase the resources devoted to implementing evaluation results. During the earlier, formal communication phase, time was not available to help managers with implementation. However, as evaluations became more complex and wider in scope, and as program managers' trust of the evaluators increased, more and more managers requested implementation assistance.

As the number of presentations per evaluation increased, the cost/benefit ratio of formal reports (which often took three to four months to complete) began to be questioned. The evaluation teams had demonstrated their technical competency and their ability to contribute to program effectiveness; consequently, reports were no longer needed to prove their professionalism. Concurrently, more time was needed to prepare and make high-quality, high-impact presentations. There was also a growing project backlog. A decision was made to write reports only when project circumstances dictated, rather than on a routine basis. These circumstances included (1) evaluation projects that produced insights of particular value to audiences outside the agency (for example, the most common deficiencies found in new product approval applications), (2) projects that produced methodologies valuable to other evaluators and analysts, and (3) the need to demonstrate to higher headquarters and other agency "watchers" that the agency was conducting meaningful program and activity evaluations.

Customized Communication. Entering the third phase of communicating evaluation results, the FDA had enough experience to feel and see the difference between the previous two phases but not enough to describe its total impact. This third phase became known as customized or "client-centered" communication, since it was built on the premise that communication activities must be based on client needs and preferences, not on presenter needs. Although this concept sounds (and is) remarkably simple, it is often difficult to implement. Frequently, analysts underestimate the time and effort needed to accurately determine client preferences, or they assume that the "messages" of their brilliant work will be communicated regardless of the communication method, or they are simply incapable of understanding the situation's behavioral dimensions.

One way to appreciate the character of the client-centered phase is to compare it with the earlier phases. Table 1 presents the important presentation and documentation characteristics of each of the three communication phases.

Client-centered communication can also be demonstrated in the form of anecdotes. The three examples described below show the diversity and orientation of this approach.

The Agency Analyst. After a major effort, an agency analyst determined the validity of the inspectional strategy in use in one of the agency's largest programs. The insights gained from the evaluation's initial aspects were counterintuitive and startling. The analyst and his supervisor immediately recognized the potential importance of these insights and suspected that future research would produce even more thought-provoking discoveries.

They developed a plan for sharing the early findings and engaging the affected parties in an evolutionary discovery process. The plan involved a "traveling road show" where these findings were presented. The audience was asked to critique the work and to suggest additional questions and avenues of inquiry. The program was managed by a matrix of managers spread across the country. The analyst made more than thirty presentations at all agency levels and across the country.

The results were truly remarkable. A new inspectional strategy emerged and became an integral part of the agency's operation. Support for the new strategy was nearly universal (the new strategy would have generated a great deal of resistance and probably failed if the agency's front line employees had not understood and accepted it). The agency's chief executive used part of the "traveling road show" in his own presentations to demonstrate the capabilities of the agency's managers and the efficiency and effectiveness of the program improved.

Table 1. Three Phases of Communicating Evaluation Results

	Presentation	Documentation
Phase I	A. In person B. Large charts C. Large audience D. Single shot E. Formal (lecture with questions)	A. Formal report (peer reviewed)
Phase II	A. In person B. Large and small (desk top) charts C. Variously sized audiences D. Multiple shots E. Conversational	A. Formal report (considered but not mandatory) B. Informal documentation (memos, annotated presentation charts)
Phase III	A. In person (usually but not exclusively; for example, video tape) B. Variety of audio visual equipment (for example, large and small charts/ computers/video tape) C. Variously sized audiences D. Multiple shots E. Tailored to client's preferred style of interaction and the presentation environment	A. Formal report (only if cost-effective) B. Informal documentation (notes, annotated presentation charts, video tape, computer programs, and so on)

The Agency Chief. During a period of budget retrenchment, the agency's new chief operating officer asked what evaluation staff members were doing to help ensure the most efficient and effective use of a particular program's resources. The request produced some feelings of anxiety, as staff members felt that they were being asked to justify their jobs. Even though staff members had valuable information to share, the new executive was inclined to "take control" of presentations whenever they covered topics he felt were not particularly relevant to pressing agency issues and problems. Also, scheduled meetings with the executive often suffered from multiple outside interruptions that demanded his immediate attention. Staff members needed a way to communicate their awareness, interest, and responsiveness in a presentation environment fraught with unexpected crises.

The solution proved to be a "random entry" presentations driven by menus. Although this approach is common to some interactive computer systems, it had not previously been used as a communication technique during a verbal presentation. The chief operating officer was presented with a menu of several program aspects that the evaluators had previously examined and were prepared to discuss. He selected several areas for presentation and engaged the evaluators in a constructive exchange of ideas and thoughts about additional areas of study. The menu-driven presentation was a success. It provided the perfect mechanism for eliciting the executive's specific interests, educating him, and demonstrating the staff's knowledge and contributions to improved program performance, all within the executive's limited time frame.

The Agency Evaluator. An agency evaluator, working on a particularly sensitive program area, was asked to address a senior field executive committee about his study design and progress to date. The managers were arriving at the agency's headquarters from all over the country for an intense, three-day marathon meeting covering a variety of critical issues and operational problems. The evaluator was excited about this rare opportunity to talk to so many key, geographically dispersed stakeholders at one time, until he learned that his presentation was scheduled for the third day immediately after lunch. He was concerned that the worn-out, sleepy managers would not give his evaluation the attention he felt it deserved.

His solution was to program the evaluation results he thought would be of personal interest to each committee member on a lightweight personal computer. The evaluator was able to organize his study results on both a national and regional basis. The regional breakout conformed to the geographical areas managed by each of the committee members. The computer could be easily transported to the meeting site (some miles from the evaluator's office) and then attached to a state-of-the-art device that projected the small computer's screen onto a larger screen that the entire committee could see. The evaluator employed an interactive, graphic systems approach. Thus, he could introduce his topic and then let the committee decide which regions of the country they were most interested in examining. When he showed the results of one committee member's region, the others became excited and wanted to see how their respective regions compared. Not only were the managers taken by the technology, they were excited about seeing large amounts of data on programs they were personally responsible for organized and presented in such an efficient, comprehensible manner. The technology and the customized presentation, each powerful in its own right, were synergistic when coupled together.

The presentation approach was clearly successful. After the meeting, several committee members expressed their personal appreciation to the evaluator and their willingness to support the evaluation in any way they could.

In summary, client-centered communication of evaluation results is here to stay partly because it increases the probability of evaluation impact and partly because clients who have experienced it will settle for nothing less effective. Now, we must consider the potential of communication techniques previously reserved for advertising agencies, speech writers, and the theatre.

Networking: An Investment That Pays Dividends

In-house evaluators are likely to find that network developments are effective mechanisms for increasing the eventual impact of their analytical work. In this setting, the term *network* is used to describe working relationships between the evaluator and all other interested parties. Networking also refers to the working relationships that an evaluator may need to establish among the various parties. Networking is particularly valuable in large, complex organizations where the power is widely distributed and where many parties have the ability to sabotage evaluation results implementation but few, if any, have the power to ensure it.

Frequently, the establishment of effective networks requires substantial effort. The inexperienced or analytically focused analyst may not recognize networking's value, seeing it in terms of unnecessary "ego soothing." However, if the evaluator sees result implementation as an important dimension of the evaluation process, networking's advantages will be obvious. The advantages described below are based on the experiences of in-house evaluation staff members over a ten-year period.

1. An evaluator who has established a network with the various "players" interested in the program is more likely to develop a thorough, accurate sense of that program's reality (something a complex program's manager does not have but is likely to respect). Unless evaluators are already intimately familiar with every facet of their programs, they will need these perspectives to design and efficiently conduct their work and to ensure that their findings are used.

2. Evaluators with networks can identify and gain access to all of the available automated and hard copy data relating to their programs. In part, this is because program managers may not control some of these data sources or even be aware of them. By networking with stakeholders at various levels, evaluators can reduce their dependency on just one or two key people. Not having to go through organizational layers to hit "pay dirt" also speeds up the data search process.

3. Evaluations are often viewed with suspicion (and sometimes hostility) by managers who have never experienced one, or who have had a negative experience. Often, these suspicions make managers cautious about sharing data and insights, thereby handicapping or crippling the evaluation. Initially, the FDA's evaluation staff established formal teams to conduct evaluations. In theory, these teams provided more staffing so that evaluations could be done more quickly and effectively. In reality, team members were frequently directed by their organization to keep an eye on the evaluator (damage control). As evaluators gained acceptance

and credibility among agency managers, the formal team concept came to be viewed as too costly (especially in an era of diminishing resources). It has since been replaced with a less formal networking process. The network assures interested organizations that they will be kept informed of the evaluators' activities, findings, and insights on a "real time" basis. This both decreases managerial concern and increases support of the evaluators' efforts.

4. A comprehensive network ensures that an evaluation can be completed even if the initial client who commissioned it is no longer interested or available. Recently, a manager decided to retire midway through the evaluation he had commissioned. Since a number of other agency managers with various aspects of control over the program (for example, the program manager's supervisor or district directors from a separate component of the agency) were involved and supportive, the evaluators were able to finish their work and substantially impact the program. If active networking had not been used from the very beginning, the evaluation would have either died or been significantly delayed while another sponsor was identified and cultivated.

5. Networking increases the likelihood of timely and complete evaluation result implementation. Quick, cheap evaluation studies are meaningless if their recommendations are not implemented, or implemented incorrectly, due to misunderstandings and mistrust. Even when an evaluation is done for the head of a major organization, it cannot be assumed that its results will automatically be implemented.

A former cabinet secretary with substantial private sector experience observed that, although he was the department head, the department's employees were capable of delaying or even stopping any substantive policy changes they did not agree with. He concluded that a government executive or manager cannot unilaterally control the development and administration of policy. Therefore, government executives have "to learn to become one of a large number of players in a floating crap game, rather than the leader of a well-organized casino" (Blumenthal, 1979). The same can be said for evaluators and their primary clients. Effective networking gives implementors a sense of ownership in the evaluation's design and execution. And with ownership comes cooperation and support.

6. Networks developed through one evaluation can often be capitalized on when conducting subsequent studies, thus making those efforts even more timely and inexpensive. In some federal agencies, program implementation is actually carried out in field offices across the country or through state agencies associated with the federal program. If these geographically distributed managers feel that a particular evaluation has been a positive experience, they are likely to be willing participants in future evaluations.

Although the six networking benefits described above may be compelling, there are some potential barriers to be considered. In the FDA's experience, the following are the most frequently encountered and the most difficult to overcome.

Scheduling Frustrations. Since networks typically include managers with busy schedules, it is frequently difficult to schedule meetings at appropriate points in the evaluation. Since it is vital that managers feel that evaluators are dedicated to keeping them informed, evaluators may need to develop such alternative involvement techniques as brief phone updates, periodic notes (describing activities and offering to answer questions), and communicating through those who *do* have routine access to managers.

Fear of Rejection or Conflict. Individual analysts may avoid contacting important network members for fear of rejection or poor treatment. These fears are usually unfounded. In most instances, the network link can be established instantly by simply saying, "We are doing an analysis of the XYZ program. Do you want to know about the study plan?" Program managers' anxieties can be further decreased by involving them in deciding the evaluation's timing. The FDA's experience has been that government line managers expect all programs to be evaluated periodically. At the same time, they believe that evaluations done at the wrong time can be not only ineffective but also impaired.

Delayed Analytical Results. Many talented analysts are inclined to focus on data bases, analytical techniques, and quantifiable results. They are frustrated by the time and effort required to establish networks, preferring to "get to the good stuff." The value of networks may only become apparent when they are needed to obtain data, avoid sabotage efforts, or implement results. Careful recruiting and positive reinforcement are needed to ensure that networking activities receive the attention they need and deserve.

One experienced (and effective) analyst summarized the costs and benefits of networking as a "pay me now, or pay me later" proposition. He argued that it was almost always cheaper to develop a network at the beginning of an evaluation than to overcome resistance during the evaluation and sell the results of the evaluation at its conclusion.

Conclusion

This chapter discussed two concepts that have proven effective in facilitating the impact, timeliness, and use of low-cost, short-term evaluations. The concepts are both mutually compatible and complementary. (For example, a client-centered approach to communication is needed to satisfy the diverse needs of network members. As clients, stakeholders, and other interested and affected parties have diverse information needs

72

that range from simple awareness to in-depth, step-by-step understanding, there is no "one size fits all" communication technique that can accommodate them all. But the creative use of alternative communication methods can help overcome the difficulties. It is not surprising that the term *network* applies to both multiple interpersonal relationships and linkages in communication.

References

Barkdoll, G. "Type III Evaluations: Consultation and Consensus." *Public Administration Review*, 1980, *42*, 174–179.
Blumenthal, M. "Candid Reflections of a Businessman in Washington." *Fortune*, January 19, 1979, pp. 36–49.

Gerald L. Barkdoll is the associate commissioner for planning and evaluation of the U.S. Food and Drug Administration and an adjunct professor at the Washington Public Affairs Center of the University of Southern California.

Douglas L. Sporn is director of the evaluation and analysis staff of the U.S. Food and Drug Administration and a program evaluation consultant to the World Health Organization.

*Evaluations must respond rapidly to legislative information
needs. In certain cases, this implies the development of
methods that can provide answers even more quickly than
usual. Currently, GAO is testing three such methods: the
evaluation synthesis, the use of extant data, and the evaluation
planning review. All three methods rely heavily on past
research, all place heavy time pressures on evaluators, and
all are highly promising in terms of user satisfaction.*

Federal Evaluation in a Legislative Environment: Producing on a Faster Track

Eleanor Chelimsky

In 1980, the U.S. General Accounting Office (GAO) decided to establish a
program evaluation division. Beyond producing methodologically strong
studies, its purpose was to improve the usefulness of evaluations to legislative sponsors. One major obstacle to this goal was the length of time
required by certain evaluation methods (sometimes between two and three
years). Because of such time lags, evaluative information sometimes lost
its timeliness in a legislative context: the committee or staff member who
sponsored the study might have departed, committee interests might have
changed, or new legislation might have rendered the findings moot.
Obviously, the timing of final (and interim) products needed to dovetail
reasonably well with congressional milestones, policy cycles, and committee plans if the evaluation's findings were to prove useful.

Since its inception, a major effort has been underway in the GAO's
Program Evaluation and Methodology Division (PEMD) to find ways of
developing timely answers to legislative questions. The effort has focused
on shortening the necessary performance times and on developing or
adapting methods that can bring faster answers, while maintaining
acceptable quality levels.

C. G. Wye, H. P. Hatry (eds.). *Timely, Low-Cost Evaluation in the Public Sector.*
New Directions for Program Evaluation, no. 38. San Francisco: Jossey-Bass, Summer 1988.

PEMD is a division that today counts 115 staff members. More than 90 percent of our analysts have advanced degrees, with 60 percent having Ph.D.'s. Disciplines are varied: Academic training ranges from degrees in chemistry and mathematics through psychology and sociology, to engineering, economics, statistics, and political science. We have about forty-five studies ongoing at any one time; these have varying durations lasting from about six months to two years.

The general PEMD approach to improving congressional evaluation use has three major features: It (1) begins with a very precise understanding of the legislative sponsor's information needs, (2) builds two kinds of linkages (a *logic* linkage that attaches particular legislative information needs to particular evaluation strategies and a continuing communication linkage that improves the sponsor's awareness of how the work is progressing, what the product will be, and how legislative questions will be answered), and (3) develops new ways to answer legislative questions when resource constraints preclude the use of more typical methods.

When trying to understand an individual legislative information need, PEMD may discover, for example, that the sponsor requires a full-scale effectiveness evaluation of reauthorization hearings that are two years away. In such a case, PEMD would employ whichever traditional study design would produce the most conclusive information. But if only six to nine months were available, new ways of obtaining the information would need to be found. Working with Congress, the PEMD's most frequent resource constraint has been time. As a result, they have developed two fast-track methods for producing evaluative information and are in the process of developing a third. These methods are (1) the evaluation synthesis, (2) the use of extant data, and (3) the evaluation planning review. This chapter discusses these methods, describes their techniques, gives examples of completed work, and appraises each method's success in terms of time efficiency, costs, credibility, and sponsor satisfaction.

Evaluation Synthesis (ES)

This method was developed to respond to legislative sponsors who need effectiveness studies when not enough time is available to collect original data. The ES method is used only when a sponsor is willing to accept an analysis of existing studies as a substitute for a new, original-data evaluation. An ES determines what is actually known in a particular topic area, assesses how much confidence one may have in the various studies that make up its data base, and identifies any remaining gaps in the needed information.

The evaluation synthesis method has eight basic steps (GAO, Apr. 1983; Chelimsky and Morra, 1984):

- Identifying and negotiating the evaluation topic and specific questions to be answered with the sponsor
- Collecting evaluation studies and other empirical information to develop an archive on the topic
- Determining the study types to include and selecting those studies
- Reviewing the studies for methodological soundness
- Redetermining the ES method's appropriateness for answering the sponsor's questions
- Synthesizing the information and determining confidence levels
- Identifying any knowledge gaps that remain
- Presenting the findings.

Identifying the Topic and Questions. A key element in the ES strategy is the initial negotiating process, during which legislative sponsors and the PEMD reach an agreement on the study's specific questions, the appropriateness of the ES method for producing the needed information, the ready date of the first and final products, and the use to which the findings will be put. At this early stage, the PEMD needs assurance that there is existent data capable of answering the study's questions without the need of new, additional information, and that the questions can be answered with the allotted time and resources. Congressional staff members need to understand the forthcoming information's limitations and to agree that it is, in fact, what they need and want.

Collecting Studies. Given a policy question or questions, it is not always easy to identify which existent data are pertinent. This is a major difference between meta-analysis and evaluation synthesis. In the former, the analyst is very familiar with the data base and is searching for new questions which that base might answer. In the latter, the questions are already known, but often the range of existing studies remains vague. The search for those studies usually begins with a query to the federal and state agencies that administer the policy or program. Beyond that, unsponsored literature, both published and unpublished, is researched. It is important to ascertain how biased a collected sample may be. Ensuring that no *major* studies have been omitted is crucial to the validity of ES findings. The PEMD's solution has been to ask large groups of experts (sometimes numbering more than 100, depending on the subject area) to help them identify any relevant literature.

Selecting the Studies. Here the chief concern is identifying and controlling any potential bias sources. To mitigate this problem, the PEMD has tried to include as many different types of study designs in the ES data base as possible. Typically, the data base may include national surveys, effectiveness evaluations, case studies, process studies, document reviews, and many other quantitative and qualitative analysis examples.

Reviewing the Studies. One ES product is a soundness assessment of each individual study in the data base. All studies are appraised against basic standards for research design, conduct, analysis, and reporting. Although these standards are generally similar, they do differ somewhat, depending on the particular subject and the kinds of studies that have already been done in the area. Criteria standards are therefore developed for each PEMD study, taking into consideration the data base's particular characteristics (for example, designs employed, measures used, and questions examined). In a recent ES on drinking-age laws, the studies were rated in terms of (1) the existence and adequacy of comparison groups, (2) source data use, (3) the appropriateness and comparability of the measures used, (4) the appropriateness of methods for taking chance into account, and (5) the extent to which a study controlled for other factors and provided quantitative measures of difference.

The bias of reviewers is always a concern. The systematic application of explicit criteria helps control such bias by preventing different reviewers from using different criteria and from applying them in some instances but not others. Additionally, rating reliability is also checked.

Redetermining Appropriateness. Although preliminary evidence may seem to show that an ES can answer a sponsor's question, this sometimes turns out not to be true. For example, the PEMD collected a number of studies that attempted to estimate the size of the U.S. illegal alien population (GAO, Sept. 24, 1982). However, the estimate range was so large, the quality of the studies so questionable, and the potential explanatory factors so numerous that it became clear a new research effort would be needed. Based on this experience, the PEMD concluded that the ES method's appropriateness should always be explicitly reconfirmed.

Synthesizing the Information. After a usable set of studies has been assembled, they must be contrasted and compared. No single approach works in all cases, but the PEMD usually employs a nonquantitative approach. The nature and extent of similar findings or trends across studies are looked for and rival alternative explanations for the findings are ruled out. With one exception (GAO, Jan. 30, 1984), the PEMD has thus far been unable to use statistical aggregation techniques to combine findings from different studies. This is due to the fact that the PEMD begins with a sponsor's questions, rather than with a data base chosen to allow statistical aggregation. (That is, because of the user-driven nature of the questions addressed, the data base is often made up of disparate, fragmented evaluations.) When a researcher bases the selection of a topic for meta-analysis on its potential for producing new knowledge, the new statistical approaches can often be used. But when, as in our case, we must design backward from a legislative sponsor's question, those approaches are usually difficult to apply.

Even when studies *can* be statistically synthesized, this technique should only be used in combination with nonquantitative approaches, since the merging of quantitative and nonquantitative techniques has at least two important benefits. First, multiple evidence lines that yield complementary findings increase the likelihood of quality results. Second, studies that cannot be included in the traditional quantitative synthesis (for example, case studies, nonquantitative aggregate studies, expert judgments, and process-oriented studies) can help to explain quantitative findings. At the very least, they can suggest possible explanations, which can then be treated as hypotheses.

Identifying Gaps and Presenting Findings. Documenting the fact that some legislative questions cannot be answered using available evidence is an important part of the ES product. It helps set the stage for needed new research. At the same time, it gives legislative decision makers a better idea of how complete the information is on which they must currently rely for making policy. In a recent ES on the management of hazardous waste, perhaps the most important finding was that estimates previously considered accurate were fallible (GAO, Feb. 18, 1987).

Individual chapters in the PEMD's synthesis reports usually correspond to the legislative sponsor's questions. For each question, both what is known and what is not known is highlighted.

Examples of Completed Work. Twelve of the PEMD's completed evaluation syntheses are listed in Table 1. Often, the ES method has served to answer questions about program operations. For example, in the ES on the Education of All Handicapped Children Act the study's purpose was to determine how many people needed program service (GAO, Sept. 30, 1981). Existing studies provided an estimate of which handicapping conditions were underrepresented and at which grade and age levels.

The ES method has also been used to answer questions about program effects. The PEMD's report on the Comprehensive Employment and Training Act (CETA), for example, examined the effects of CETA programs on disadvantaged adult enrollees (GAO, June 14, 1982). That report provided legislative users with estimates of wages earned and time employed, public benefits received, and private sector employment of CETA participants before and after they participated in the program. (For other examples of program effects usage, see GAO, Jan. 30, 1984; Mar. 16, 1987.) The PEMD's study on chemical warfare is an example of answering questions about the state of knowledge in an area (GAO, Apr. 29, 1983).

The ES method has also been used to compare performances between two or more programs. For example, the PEMD's report on block grants addressed the question of whether the poor and other disadvantaged groups have been served equally under block grants and categorical programs (GAO, Sept. 23, 1982).

Table 1. IPE/PEMD Applications of Evaluation Synthesis
as of August 15, 1987

The Handicapped
- Disparities Still Exist in Who Gets Special Education
(IPE-81-1, September 1981)

Manpower Training
- CETA Programs for Disadvantaged Adults—What Do We Know About the Enrollees, Services, and Effectiveness?
(IPE-82-2, June 1982)

Entitlement Programs
- Lessons Learned from Past Block Grants: Implications for Congressional Oversight
(IPE-82-8, September 1982)

Health Care
- The Elderly Should Benefit from Expanded Home Health Care but Increasing These Services Will Not Insure Cost Reduction
(IPE-83-1, December 1982)

Public Assistance
- CWEP's Implementation Results to Date Raise Questions About the Administration's Proposed Mandatory Workfare Program
(PEMD-84-2, April 1984)

- WIC Evaluations Provide Some Favorable but No Conclusive Evidence on the Effects Expected for the Special Supplemental Program for Women, Infants, and Children
(PEMD-84-4, January 1984)

Defense
- Chemical Warfare: Many Unanswered Questions
(IPE-83-6, April 1983)

Housing
- Housing Allowances: An Assessment of Program Participation and Effects
(PEMD-86-3, February 1986)

Environment
- The Nation's Water: Key Unanswered Questions About the Quality of Rivers and Streams
(PEMD-86-6, September 1986)

- Hazardous Waste: Uncertainties of Existing Data
(PEMD-87-11, February 1987)

Immigration
- Illegal Aliens: Limited Research Suggests Illegal Aliens May Displace Native Workers
(PEMD-86-9, April 1986)

Transportation
- Drinking Age Laws: An Evaluation Synthesis of Their Impact on Highway Safety
(PEMD-87-10, March 1987)

Note: GAO's Program Evaluation and Methodology Division was called the Institute for Program Evaluation until 1983.

Assessment. ES studies are meant to be performed by one or two staff members who have either specialized expertise in the topic area or access to such expertise. While ES is a feasible method in either case, staff level expertise results in major performance efficiency at almost every stage of the process.

Costs vary widely. In thoroughly studied, mature research areas where staff level expertise is available, these studies can be produced very economically. However, when the work has to begin from zero, when repeated study searches have to be initiated, or when typical job hazards (illness, staff transfers) intervene, they become more expensive. In general, it would be accurate to say that ES studies always cost less than studies involving original data collection. Nonetheless, the cost range underscores the importance of carefully determining the ES method's appropriateness in each case. Major factors affecting its appropriateness are (1) the research maturity of a particular topic; (2) the existence of relevant independent evaluations (at least five or six, preferably more) and other empirical work; (3) the accessibility of the literature; and (4) staff expertise in the subject. However, an ES may provide, *relative to other methods,* the most cost-effective and timely way to answer a sponsor's questions, regardless of these appropriateness factors.

Overall, the ES has proved to be an extremely useful method. It does not take the place of an original study but provides a helpful alternative. Generally, sponsors have been happy to receive their products earlier than would otherwise have been the case. The work credibility has been quite acceptable, except in areas where too few studies existed, and where now, having had more experience, the PEMD would probably not use the method.

Use of Extant Data

The PEMD has a policy to make use of extant data wherever possible when performing full-scale evaluations, in order to reduce duration and costs. They rely on federal, state, or local data to help resolve many evaluation difficulties.

Typically, the PEMD's program evaluation process is composed of five phases: a review of the substantive and methodological literature; evaluation design; data collection; data analysis; and reporting. Extant data have been important in each of the first three phases.

Review of the Literature. At the beginning of a program evaluation, a literature review is always undertaken to ensure (1) a grasp of the underlying substantive issues that have informed both the program and its legislative history, (2) an awareness of past research methods and measures that have been employed to evaluate the program, and (3) a firm basis for estimating the feasibility and usefulness of an evaluation in the given program area. Existing data are particularly helpful in regard to feasibility and usefulness.

For example, in a process evaluation of residential placement for children and youth the availability of data on the number and types of children in residential care was a major factor in ascertaining whether such a study would be feasible within time and budget constraints (GAO, June 28, 1985). Had such information not been documented, filed, retained, and accessible, it is unlikely that this study would have been possible.

In a comparative evaluation assessing the relative cost-effectiveness of reduction-in-force (RIF), furloughs, and attrition, the PEMD looked at the range of available administrative data in each federal agency's monitoring system to decide first, whether such an evaluation was possible, and second, which variables were feasible for cross-agency examination (GAO, July 24, 1985).

Evaluation Design. The availability of extant data is again a major consideration when deciding on a particular design. A quantitative case study design, for example, is much more feasible when existent national data can furnish benchmarks against which case study data can be compared. While this will not solve the generalizability (or external validity) problem affecting case study designs, it certainly helps to establish confidence in case study findings.

One PEMD evaluation used a case study design to examine the effects of the OBRA (Omnibus Budget Reconciliation Act) legislation on participants in the AFDC (Aid to Families with Dependent Children) program (GAO, July 2, 1985). Evaluators used existent data on state AFDC plan characteristics in the site selection process to ensure that the selected sites would reflect a variety of AFDC program dimensions.

The RIF/furlough/attrition design mentioned earlier used administrative data on the size, scope, and timing of RIFs to help select agencies for study. Similarly, an evaluation on the status of runaway and homeless youth made use of a system monitoring grant applications from each funded site for sample selection purposes (GAO, Sept. 26, 1987). The accessed data included site-specific information on community types (urban, suburban, or rural), years of site operation, years of federal funding, actual federal dollars requested and granted for previous and current fiscal years, administrative affiliations, number of beds, number of clients served, extent of volunteer use, major nonfederal contributors, shelter types (center run, host home, combination), major sources of referrals, and degree of networking with other agencies.

For a national defense industrial base evaluation, the PEMD made use of Defense Department administrative data to select sample case studies (GAO, Apr. 4, 1985).

Data Collection. In some cases, administrative data have furnished almost the entire basis for an evaluation. For example, an evaluation of state responses to the rising demands and costs of nursing home care used federal data to study nursing home expenditure trends by type of service (GAO, Oct. 21, 1983). State expenditure data are listed by facility type and are reported in January for each prior fiscal year. This data (much of it unpublished) permitted the examination of expenditure trends for services over time and across states.

Similarly, administrative data played a major role in the CETA program's ES discussed earlier. Three types of data were used: data on participant characteristics (to address targeting), financial reports (to address expenditures), and program status reports (to address both the mix of services and placement rates). These data were required to be submitted by prime sponsors (local administering bodies) to the Department of Labor on a quarterly or yearly basis; reports were broken down separately for each CETA title.

Assessment. Overall, it is clear that an evaluator's ability to respond to questions about program effectiveness or status in an appropriate time frame and at reasonable cost is dependent on the availability and quality of existing data. This does not mean that, were these data lacking, there would be no other way of responding to specific legislative questions. But it does mean that when the data are both accessible and adequate, evaluations will be more realistic, more easily and better specified, more rapidly and inexpensively performed, wider in coverage or richer in detail, and more powerful than they could be without them, time and costs being equal.

In general, the use of extant data is free and represents a net savings over collecting original data. In some cases, administrative data represent a unique good in that, because time has passed, it would have been impossible to substitute new data for them.

The use of extant data conveys two major benefits to an evaluation: time saved and uncertainty decreased. In many cases, had it not been for the existence of these data, we would not have been able to finish an evaluation on time or have felt justified at the design stage in thinking that the evaluation was feasible.

The issue of credibility is of great importance. All extant data are not usable data. In one case, the PEMD had anticipated using data from the Social Security Administration's Retirement History Survey to analyze retirement patterns among the elderly. The data's quality proved to be so poor that both its use and the evaluation were abandoned (GAO, July 6, 1982).

Data access can be a problem on occasion. In most cases, data are public and agencies have facilitated their use; in other cases, agencies have withheld data until their usefulness had expired; in still other instances, agencies have classified the data so that they could not be used in an unclassified study.

Staff awareness of data bases and staff understanding of the potential evaluative uses of administrative data are both essential to making the best use of existent data. These data are important adjuncts of an evaluation in their own right, and of great value in meeting the time frames of legislative sponsors.

Evaluation Planning Review (EPR)

Both the ES and the use of existent data are, in essence, shorter-track substitutes for traditional methods used in *retrospective* evaluations. The EPR, for its part, tries to expand the methodological tools used in *prospective* evaluations. While it is true that front-end analysis is recognized (in the Evaluation Research Society's standards) as one of the six conventional evaluation approaches, few methods exist for routinely performing it (see ERS Standards Committee, 1982).

The PEMD's evaluation planning review wanted to systematically apply existing evaluative information to some new legislative proposal, either prior to its formal congressional introduction or prior to its formal promulgation as an executive branch program. Evaluators can contribute greatly to program quality by clarifying the reasoning behind program goals, by identifying the problems to be addressed, by selecting the best intervention point and the intervention type most likely to succeed. They can do this by bringing an understanding of similar programs' past effects to the design and development of new ones.

The EPR therefore seeks to operate before agendas are set. However, the speed with which new programs are sometimes introduced means that evaluative information cannot always be mobilized in time to be useful. New bills can become law at a hectic pace. Recently, Senator Moynihan complained that the provisions of the Gramm-Rudman-Hollings bill were still being "tinkered with" while he was preparing to vote on it on the floor. This rapid tempo signifies the need for a useful short-term (three to four months) method that can intervene between the time that a decision is taken to propose a new program and the time that program is introduced.

The PEMD's experience with EPRs is extremely limited. They evaluated two proposed Senate bills focusing on teenage pregnancy (GAO, July 21, 1986) and a second application comparing two legislative proposals to improve catastrophic health care coverage (GAO, July 30, 1987). Both applications sought to reveal any legislative implications that could be drawn from existing knowledge about the problem and from past efforts to solve it.

The PEMD's methodology in the teenage pregnancy study involved four major steps:

1. They examined the two Senate bills to determine the nature of

the problem the programs were intended to address, the activities and operations of each program package, and the proposals' assumptions about how their strategies were intended to achieve their policy objectives.

2. They identified the most important published empirical work on teenage pregnancy as well as previous efforts to address it.

3. They evaluated findings from those previous efforts, taking research characteristics and data quality into account, in order to determine whether the proposed programs were likely to achieve their policy objectives and to determine likely problems of implementation, operation, and management.

4. They compared these findings to the features of the two pieces of proposed legislation.

Proposals. The key features of each bill in order were analyzed, in order to select the most appropriate evidence to review. The proposed eligibility criteria for services, service providers, and recipients meant that the reviews had to focus on two kinds of projects: those targeted to *prevention,* and those targeted to comprehensive postpregnancy *services.* These eligibility criteria expanded the PEMD's estimates of the target populations. Policy objective models were constructed for each bill. These defined the interest outcomes to which the PEMD restricted its review of prior efforts.

Identifying Research. The search for the most important studies began with a broadly focused examination of thirteen computerized bibliographic files. The PEMD wanted to find as many relevant documents as possible, but restricted its search to those published after 1980.

The computerized searches yielded more than 1,100 references, many with abstracts. The items that appeared to be the most relevant were classified into four main categories: reports of prevention and service projects, summaries of such projects and discussions of general policy, research on the size and scope of the issue, and summaries of research on the antecedents and consequences of teenage pregnancy.

Next, the research studies' bibliographies and reviews were reviewed to identify any studies that might have been missed in the computerized searches. At the same time, nineteen experts on demography and relevant programs were contacted to identify works in progress and elicit nominations for the "most important" research. This search yielded a total of seventy documents.

Information on the prevalence of teenage pregnancy and childbearing was needed to ascertain the problem's seriousness and to estimate service needs. To this end, published literature was reviewed, birth statistics reported by the National Center for Health Statistics and others were analyzed, and income and fertility information in a number of public and private data bases were investigated.

As no reliable estimates of the number of poor pregnant or parenting teenagers were readily available, data on the characteristics that previous research had identified as being associated with the problem were examined. These included age, marital status, and educational attainment.

Evaluating Studies. Prevention or postpregnancy service project documents that reported no data on any of the bills' specified outcomes were set aside. Then, each remaining project study was rated by the information quality of its outcome measure. These separate ratings were required because some outcomes were measured with different designs within the same study. Six dimensions were adapted from the PEMD's ES methodology:

- The comparison group's similarity to the project's clients
- The adequacy of the sample size and the extent of attrition (in studies using longitudinal designs)
- The standardization of data collection procedures
- The appropriateness of the measures used to represent outcome variables
- The adequacy of statistical (or other) methods used to control validity (that is, possible influences on observed differences other than program participation)
- The presence and appropriateness of methods used to analyze the statistical significance of observed differences.

Ratings were made on a three-point scale from "unacceptable" (no information on a study method or a method so flawed that the data were probably wrong) to "acceptable" (an appropriate method with attempts to minimize endemic problems). All ratings were based on published materials that often did not fully disclose the evaluation procedures.

These dimensional ratings were then combined to judge the overall acceptability of data on each outcome variable for inclusion in our synthesis of results.

Synthesizing Results. In order to compare information on prior efforts with the two bills' proposals, the projects were characterized by types of service and service delivery. Three postpregnancy service project types were identified on the basis of academic and vocational service provisions and primary service delivery settings (health facility or school). Prevention projects were characterized by the service components identified in the PEMD's general review, as well as by some of the service delivery characteristics proposed for the comprehensive service program. These projects were too few and too diverse to permit convenient grouping. Studies that had no comparison data were excluded.

The PEMD's second EPR focused on proposals for improving "catastrophic" health care insurance, using the same method described above. That is, proposals were analyzed, prior research was identified, catastrophic insurance experiences in five states were evaluated, and the results were synthesized.

Assessment. It is too soon to provide a realistic appraisal of the EPR's pros and cons. However, based on the PEMD's limited experience, the method seems to have real promise.

Costs were very low, due to short timelines and the use of existent data. In both studies, the work was completed on time, congressional staff members were very interested in the method, and the findings were used immediately. The sponsor of the teenage pregnancy study accepted the PEMD's conclusion that an innovative program featuring sound comprehensive evaluation and dissemination was needed, and is incorporating these findings and recommendations in new legislation. It is too early to speak about use for the catastrophic health care study, but findings on the problems experienced by the elderly when paying for prescription drugs have already resulted in Medicare legislation draft change.

These two studies emphasize the importance of choosing EPR topics carefully. The effort will always be arduous at best: much overtime and weekend work is normally required, due to short time periods and large work loads. If the topic is a highly publicized, much-debated one and its timing is such that work takes place in an end-of-session atmosphere where legislation is moving *very* fast, then the study's credibility can be jeopardized, and with it the work's ultimate usefulness. The point is that time is already at a premium; when choosing the topic, it is important not to restrict it further.

EPRs *must* be timely, and to be timely they must be at least somewhat selective. That is, the attempt to be comprehensive or exhaustive (as with an ES) in reviewing all possible studies, projects, or research is not appropriate.

The EPR has three important advantages. First, it allows evaluation to make policy contributions embodying the best accumulated information. Second, legislative committee staff members obtain expert design assistance for new programs, assistance that can ultimately help convince other legislators of these programs' validity and likely success. Third, by providing a before-the-fact understanding of how programs might work, EPRs render an invaluable public service. They help strengthen programs that are not optimally structured and validate the basic soundness of what is to be undertaken.

References

Chelimsky, E., and Morra, L. G. "Evaluation Synthesis for the Legislative User." In W. H. Yeaton and P. M. Wortman (eds.), *Issues in Data Synthesis.* New Directions for Program Evaluation, no. 24. San Francisco: Jossey-Bass, 1984.

ERS Standards Committee. "Evaluation Research Society Standards for Program Evaluation." In P. H. Rossi (ed.), *Standards for Evaluation Practice.* New Directions for Program Evaluation, no. 15. San Francisco: Jossey-Bass, 1982.

U.S. General Accounting Office. *Disparities Still Exist in Who Gets Special Education.* GAO/IPE-81-1, Sept. 30, 1981.

U.S. General Accounting Office. *CETA Programs for Disadvantaged Adults—What Do We Know About Their Enrollees, Services, and Effectiveness?* GAO/IPE-82-2, June 14, 1982.

U.S. General Accounting Office. *Data from the Retirement History Survey.* Letter to Director, Bureau of the Census, GAO/IPE-82-5, July 6, 1982.

U.S. General Accounting Office. *Lessons Learned from Past Block Grants: Implications for Congressional Oversight.* GAO/IPE-82-8, Sept. 23, 1982.

U.S. General Accounting Office. *Problems and Options in Estimating the Size of the Illegal Alien Population.* GAO/IPE-82-9, Sept. 24, 1982.

U.S. General Accounting Office. *Chemical Warfare: Many Unanswered Questions.* GAO/IPE-83-6, Apr. 29, 1983.

U.S. General Accounting Office. *The Evaluation Synthesis.* Methods Paper no. 1. Apr. 1983.

U.S. General Accounting Office. *Medicaid and Nursing Home Care: Cost Increases and the Need for Services Are Creating Problems for the States and the Elderly.* GAO/IPE-84-1, Oct. 21, 1983.

U.S. General Accounting Office. *WIC Evaluations Provide Some Favorable but No Conclusive Evidence on the Effects Expected for the Special Supplemental Program for Women, Infants, and Children.* GAO/PEMD-84-4, Jan. 30, 1984.

U.S. General Accounting Office. *Assessing Production Capabilities and Constraints in the Defense Industrial Base.* GAO/PEMD-85-3, Apr. 4, 1985.

U.S. General Accounting Office. *Residential Care: Patterns of Child Placement in Three States.* GAO/PEMD-85-2, June 28, 1985.

U.S. General Accounting Office. *An Evaluation of the 1981 AFDC Changes: Final Report.* GAO/PEMD-85-4, July 2, 1985.

U.S. General Accounting Office. *Reduction in Force Can Sometimes Be More Costly Than Attrition and Furlough.* GAO/PEMD-85-6, July 24, 1985.

U.S. General Accounting Office. *Teenage Pregnancy: 500,000 Births a Year but Few Tested Programs.* GAO/PEMD-86-16BR, July 21, 1986.

U.S. General Accounting Office. *Hazardous Waste: Uncertainties of Existing Data.* GAO/PEMD-87-11BR, Feb. 18, 1987.

U.S. General Accounting Office. *Drinking Age Laws: An Evaluation Synthesis of Their Impact on Highway Safety.* GAO/PEMD-87-10, Mar. 16, 1987.

U.S. General Accounting Office. *Medicare: Catastrophic Illness Insurance.* GAO/PEMD-87-21BR, July 30, 1987.

U.S. General Accounting Office. *Federally Supported Centers Provide Needed Services for Runaways and Homeless Youths.* GAO/IPE-83-7, Sept. 26, 1987.

Eleanor Chelimsky, director of the U.S. General Accounting Office's Program Evaluation and Methodology Division, has been conducting studies of individual government programs for Congress since 1980. She came to the GAO after ten years with the MITRE Corporation, where she directed program evaluations, policy analysis, and research management. She was a Fulbright Scholar in Paris, past president of the Evaluation Research Society, and recipient of the 1982 Myrdal Award for Government and the GAO Distinguished Service Award for 1985.

Index

A

Adult geriatric and psychiatric facilities study, as state evaluation, 42–44
Agency analyst, and client-centered communication, 66–67
Agency chief, and client-centered communication, 67–68
Agency evaluator, and client-centered communication, 68–69
Alternatives analysis, as performance auditing, 29
American Evaluation Association, 1
American Institute of Certified Public Accountants (AICPA), 22–23
Arrowsmith, D. S., 22, 24–25, 35
Auditing, definition of, 22

B

Barkdoll, G., 64–65, 72
Barnes, R. M., 29, 35
Blue Cross/Blue Shield taxation study, as state evaluation, 42, 44–45, 46
Blumenthal, M., 70, 72
Braskamp, L. A., 1, 5
Brown, R. D., 1, 5
Bryk, A. A., 1, 5
Budget agency, and state evaluation placement, 41
Budget calendar, and state evaluation, 38

C

Chelimsky, E., 74, 85
Citizen survey, 8, 14; sample questionnaire, 15
Client-centered communication, as evaluation phase, 66–69
Collecting studies, as step in ES method, 75
Communication, 64–69; three phases of, in evaluation, 67
Comparative analysis, as performance auditing, 29

Comprehensive Employment and Training Act (CETA), 77, 81
Comptroller General of the United States, 60, 61
Contract evaluation, 8, 10–14; and sample objectives, 12; sample report, 13
Credibility, and evaluators, 59–60
Customized communication, as evaluation phase, 66–69
Cycles in government, and evaluators, 59

D

Data collection, use of, in evaluation, 80–81
Design of evaluation, and use of extant data, 80
Discrete evaluation, definition of, 38
Documentation: as federal communication, 64–65; as performance auditing, 28–29

E

Education of All Handicapped Children Act, 77
EPR method. *See* Evaluation planning review method
ERS Standards Committee, 82, 85
ES method. *See* Evaluation synthesis method
Evaluating studies, in EPR method study, 84
Evaluation: of federal government in executive environment, 63–72; of federal government in legislative environment, 73–86; of local government in executive environment, 7–20; of local government in legislative environment, 21–35; of state government in executive environment, 37–48; of state government in legislative environment, 49–61
Evaluation dimensions, 64

New York Legislative Commission on Expenditure Review, 3

Northern Illinois Univeristy (NIU), engineering program study at, 56–58

O

Objectives program, 8; and sample evaluations, 10, 11

Observation: as data collection method, 55–56; as performance auditing, 28

Office of the County Auditor, 33, 35

P

Performance, definition of, 22

Performance auditing, 8, 14–17, 22–35; categories of, 24–25; definition of, 22; and elements of reports, 27; examples of, 30–35; factors influencing, 26–27; methodology of, 27–30; of organizations, 24; phases of, 27; in politics, 30; possibilities for 25–27; the process of, 27; professional standards of, 22–23; sample observation form, 17; value and practicality of, 23–25

Perspective of government, and evaluators, 59

Politics, in state evaluation, 39–40

POWER approach, for reports, 54

Presentation, as federal communication, 64–66

Presenting findings, as step in ES method, 77

Principles, of federal evaluation, 63

Process dimension, in evaluation, 64

Program Evaluation and Methodology Division (PEMD) of GAO, 73–86

Proposals, in EPR method study, 83

Q

Questionnaire: as data collection method, 55–56; as performance auditing, 28

R

Redetermining appropriateness, as step in ES method, 76

Results delay, as barrier to networking, 71

Reviewing studies, as step in ES method, 76

S

Saxe, L., 1, 5

Scheduling frustrations, as barrier to networking, 71

Selecting studies, as step in ES method, 75

Silkman, R. H., 3, 5

Standards for performance auditing, 22–23

Standards for state evaluation sections, 37–38

State evaluation in executive environment, 37–48; and budget calendar, 38; convergence of politics and evaluations in, 39–40; and importance of placement within budget agency, 41; and outside participants on study teams, 40–41; section studies for, 41–45; and uncomplicated cost-efficient methods, 38–39; usefulness of section studies for, 46–47

State evaluation in legislative environment, 49–61; context of legislative evaluation in, 50–51; Illinois effort as, 51–56; and implications for evaluators, 59–60; NIU engineering program study as, 56–58

Studies, of state evaluation sections, 41–45

Study teams. *See* Teams.

Summative evaluation, 50–51

Surveys, as performance auditing, 28

Synthesizing information, as step in ES method, 76–77

Synthesizing results, in EPR method study, 84

T

Tables of organization, as performance auditing, 29

Task dimension, in evaluation, 64

Teams, and state evaluation, 40–41

Techniques of local evaluation, 8